UNSEDUCED AND UNSHAKEN

The Place of Dignity in a Young Woman's Choices

Rosalie de Rosset

MOODY PUBLISHERS

CHICAGO

© 2012 by
ROSALIE DE ROSSET

Edited by Elizabeth Cody Newenhuyse
Interior design: Kathryn Joachim
Cover design: DogEared Design
Cover image: Kirk DouPonce and Shutterstock 4956793

Library of Congress Cataloging-in-Publication Data

Rosset, Rosalie de.
    Unseduced and unshaken : the place of dignity in young women's choices / Rosalie de Rosset, general editor and author.
        p. cm.
    Includes bibliographical references.
    ISBN 978-0-8024-0564-7
    1. Women—Conduct of life. 2. Dignity-—Religious aspects-—Christianity. 3. Christianity and culture. 4. Women-—Religious life. I. Title.
    BJ1610.R67 2012
    248.8'43--dc23

                                                            2012020942

We hope you enjoy this book from Moody Publishers. Our goal is to provide high-quality, thought-provoking books and products that connect truth to your real needs and challenges. For more information on other books and products written and produced from a biblical perspective,
go to www.moodypublishers.com or write to:

Moody Publishers
820 N. LaSalle Boulevard
Chicago, IL 60610

Moody Publishers is committed to caring wisely for God's creation and uses recycled paper whenever possible. The paper in this book consists of 10 percent post-consumer waste.

3 5 7 9 10 8 6 4 2

Printed in the United States of America

*This book is dedicated to the hundreds of wonderful young women
I have met in my classroom for over forty years, women whose stories,
joys and sorrows, insights and questions have been the inspiration
for this book. I will always remember the gift of their presence
in my life and wish for them and all women the enduring knowledge
and experience of the love of Christ who took women seriously.*

CONTENTS

About the Contributors 9

Introduction 11

1. Minding Your Dignity:
   "There is more to you than you know." 15
   Rosalie de Rosset
2. Finding Your Voice: Knowing and Being Known 35
   Pam MacRae
3. Longing: From Disparity to Desire 55
   Linda Haines
4. "Everything Is Theological" 75
   Rosalie de Rosset
5. Distracted or Dignified?: "Solid or Ghostly" 95
   Rosalie de Rosset
6. Mindful or Mindless: A Theology of Play 117
   Rosalie de Rosset
7. Reading as a Spiritual Exercise 137
   Rosalie de Rosset
8. Sexual Dignity: Not by Accident 157
   Linda Haines
9. A Theology of Modesty: Naked yet Unashamed 181
   Stacie Parlee-Johnson
10. Is It Worth It? Is He Worthy? 201
    Rosalie de Rosset

Appendix 1: It Shouldn't Be Easy 213
Appendix 2: "So Much from So Little" 217
Notes 223
Resources 235
Acknowledgments 239

ABOUT THE CONTRIBUTORS

Rosalie A. de Rosset: Rosalie has been a professor at Moody Bible Institute for forty-two years where she teaches English, homiletics, and literature. Prior to becoming a teacher, she worked at WMBI as a scriptwriter and occasional host of radio programs. She has the BA in English from Bryan College in Dayton, Tennessee; the MA in English from Northeastern Illinois University; the MDiv from Trinity Evangelical Divinity School; and the PhD in English from the University of Illinois at Chicago.

In addition to being a professor, Rosalie speaks to groups including churches, seminars, conferences, and college chapels. She has also spoken in Hawaii, New Zealand, Peru, and Russia. Over the years she has appeared on Moody Broadcasting Network programs as a guest, and she serves as the cohost of the Midday Connection Book Club. She has had articles and book reviews published in various Christian publications, and has written chapters for two Moody publications. The daughter of career missionaries, Rosalie was born and raised in Peru, South America. She resides in Chicago.

Linda R. Haines: MA, LMFT, CADC, LCPC. Linda was a journalist and freelance writer for a number of years before becoming a therapist. She did her graduate work at Loyola University in counseling psychology and has been in private practice in Chicago for over thirty years doing individual, couple, and family therapy with a sub-specialty in addictions. She also works in a mental health clinic in Evanston, Illinois.

Stacie Parlee-Johnson: Stacie earned her bachelor's degree in Bible and theology from Moody Bible Institute and her master of education from Grand Valley State University. She is currently a freshman English teacher in the Chicago public school system. She and her husband, Dr. Marcus Johnson, live in the Chicago area.

Pam MacRae: Pam is Assistant Professor in the Pastoral Studies Department teaching in the area of ministry to women. She has been involved in ministry to women for over thirty years in church ministry, retreats, and parachurch ministries. She did her undergraduate and graduate work at Moody Bible Institute and is a doctoral candidate at Bethel Seminary for a doctorate of ministry. She and her husband have two adult daughters and live in the Chicago area.

INTRODUCTION

I t takes so much strength to be unseduced by the culture," said one of my female students during a class discussion. Another one added, "No one wants to be different." And, as a group, the class agreed that they often didn't have a clue "how to respond when they were caught between the culture and their faith." As one young woman put it, "If the church doesn't teach us, we too often turn to the mainstream culture."

The book before you is written primarily for just such young Christian women—though, of course, a good bit of the material applies to a broader audience. With four decades of exposure to this group, I have heard their questions and needs and know their longing for conversation and guidance, for principles and not just for simple how-to's. I am also aware they are trying to make their way as Christians in a complicated and confusing world. A review of a classic movie led me to the word "dignity," a concept I couldn't stop thinking about and one I have seldom seen addressed. I began to see how central dignity, at first a formal-sounding word, was to Christian personhood, in this case womanhood, and so, its definition and significance forms the basis for my first chapter.

That was the beginning. Then I began to gather the materials I use in class or at conferences that consistently interests my audiences, material that seems to hit a nerve, and that addresses ongoing problems of the spirit.

And so, this book has emerged, an eclectic mixture of subjects I think are important in considering the dignified life. The content is more conceptual than how-to as I believe philosophical foundations are necessary to intelligent, knowing living. I am also convinced that naming and understanding our human dilemmas precedes application and is necessary to the ability to make conscious choices, to respond clearheadedly instead of just reacting to or passively accommodating one's surroundings. To understand personal responsibility is eminently practical.

While I love to write and have done a good bit of it, I have never wanted to write a book. Some of my reasons are philosophical, some personal. Years ago, when I was in seminary, I read something C. S. Lewis wrote in an introduction to *St. Athanasius on the Incarnation* that rang true. He said if someone "must read only the new or only the old, I would advise him to read the old." The reason for this, he argued, was that "a new book is still on its trial, and the amateur is not in a position to judge it."[1] These injunctions made sense to me. I had always enjoyed old books more than new ones. So, from time to time, when someone suggested I write a book on a topic I had spoken on or taught, I referred the person to an excellent, proven source, usually older, occasionally new. In fact, I consider myself the promoter of the best of what I read and hear. I have often argued that certain authors owe me a commission.

I have also never wanted to write a book because it is a lonely, arduous exercise, and I am not a loner. I used to joke that I'd rather go for coffee. The truth is, I am more stimulated by the act of teaching or speaking than I am by writing, unless I know that the writing I'm doing (sermons and lectures) will be addressed to a live audience whose faces I can see and whom I can talk to later. That infuses the long hours of writing with color and joy.

Through the years, having been asked if I had written a book or if I could pass on my notes, I began to see that while I could recommend many books, I knew of no one source that had collected the variety of subjects I have thought and talked about for years. I also remembered hearing a prominent writer say that new writers are necessary to say the old things in new ways to a contemporary audience. Furthermore, I realized that I didn't have to do the book alone, that some subjects were better addressed by other people whose ideas I respect. Finally, I knew anything I wrote would be based on the best of what I had read myself, that I could point my audience beyond my own work to the great works I so love. In a weak moment I said yes.

I pray that this book will begin significant conversations, lead to further reading, discussion, and even disagreement. In the process of putting together the book, I decided to call upon three women who had a special interest in or had done work on a subject that fit the intent of the book. Each of these writers has a unique voice and has been rigorous in her work. No one book dealing with a variety of subjects can be exhaustive; for that reason, pertinent topics often discussed in other places are left out. Other important issues have been treated briefly in the book, but always with a view to providing invaluable resources, a significant emphasis in this manuscript. Close attention to the titles of books and articles mentioned throughout will render wonderful possibilities for self-education, theological wisdom, psychological healing, and sometimes the pure delight of beautiful reading.

Believing in the change great narrative can effect on the reader, I have incorporated the literature I love into portions of this book, sometimes as a quote at the beginning, sometimes as the basis of argument in a chapter, and often to illustrate a point. The title *Unseduced and Unshaken* is taken from John Milton's *Paradise Lost*

(Book V, l. 89) and is a description of Abdiel, the only one of the seraphim, the highest order of angels, who remained loyal to God and refused to join the rebel group who fell with Satan. The lines read: "Abdiel, faithful found;/Unshaken, unseduced, unterrified,/ His loyalty he kept."

I could wish no more for my readers.

Rosalie de Rosset

CHAPTER 1

MINDING YOUR DIGNITY

"There is more to you than you know."

BY ROSALIE DE ROSSET

DIGNITY: Formal, grave or noble bearing, conduct
or speech; nobility or elevation of character.
The quality or condition of being worthy, esteemed
or honored; inherent nobility and worth;
poise and self-respect; formal reserve or
seriousness of manner appearance, or language.[1]

She is clothed with strength and dignity. . . .

She speaks with wisdom, and faithful instruction is on her tongue.

PROVERBS 31:25–26 (NIV)

THE DIGNIFIED WOMAN

In the spring of 2011, the newest movie version of *Jane Eyre*, based on the extraordinary 1847 novel by Charlotte Brontë, opened in theaters across the country. Though there have been a number of films based on the novel throughout the years, many critics praised it. In earlier movies, some critics noted, the lead characters have often been too good-looking, the female heroine too mild-mannered, both of these representations not in line with Brontë's characterization.

I was struck by the words of two critics. Writing for Chicago's *The Reader*, J. R. Jones notes, "Casting handsome stars in the lead roles has been a chronic compromise in adapting *Jane Eyre*, whose heroine is repeatedly described as plain looking and whose hero is downright ugly." More important, however, he writes about Jane the following words: "[In *Jane Eyre*], Brontë struck a mighty blow for her gender when she created her title character and narrator, an orphaned girl who matures into a formidably self-possessed young woman; Jane's moral sensibility is so detailed, so fully realized that no reader could think her any less a person than the men surrounding her."[2] In other words, here is a woman to be taken seriously because of her character.

"A formidably self-possessed young woman with a fully realized, detailed moral sensibility." That's a description that deserves attention. I decided to look at each primary word or phrase of the sentence to remind myself exactly what they mean. It's so easy to miss the beauty of fine language. The dictionary defines two of the words as follows. *Formidable*: causing great respect, even fear; *self-possessed*: someone who has control of her longings and attendant feelings and behavior especially when under pressure. *Fully realized, detailed moral sensibility* means that Jane has developed and refined her convictions, intellect, and longings to a great capacity. She is a woman of character, what one writer calls "the inner form that makes anyone or anything what it is—whether a person, a wine or a historical record."[3]

Although I have heard speakers and leaders stress the importance of humility and honesty for women, I have heard little or no admonition to them to be spirited.

Jones is not alone in his assessment. A. O. Scott, writing for the *New York Times*, says, "Jane Eyre may lack fortune and good looks— she is famously 'small and plain' as well as 'poor and obscure'—but as the heroine of a novel, she has everything. From the very first pages . . . Jane embodies virtues that might be off-putting if they were not so persuasive. . . . She is brave, humble, spirited and honest, the kind of person readers fall in love with and believe themselves to be in their innermost hearts."[4] Here in a secular venue is a reviewer who at once acknowledges that Jane is plain and poor and contends with admiration that she is a young woman who has "everything." The everything she has, Scott says, is that she is "humble, spirited and honest." *Spirited* is a word defined as "full of or characterized by animation, vigor, or courage."[5] Scott also admits that her virtues are "off-putting if they were not so persuasive," a particularly intriguing phrase. How interesting that a contemporary, secular critic has found a plain woman to have "everything." And, I might add, how comforting and unusual. That he thinks readers "believe themselves to be [Jane] in their innermost hearts" has to be a mark of what many women and some men want to be since the reality is that few people today are like Jane. Even fewer quickly admire the Janes they meet in real life, a telling irony.

Over a period of thirty-five years, I have spoken at a great many conferences and seminars for women of all ages, but I have never seen advertised or heard a talk entitled, "How to become a formidable, self-possessed woman of fully realized moral sensibility." Although I have heard speakers and leaders stress the importance of humility and honesty for women, I have heard little or no admonition to them to be spirited, even though the definition of the word as noted above describes a commendable, even necessary attribute for a woman of character.

I can't help stopping on the last reviewer's words that Jane has virtues which are "off-putting if they were not so persuasive." I think what he means is that Jane knows her mind, a quality that is always startling, even threatening. In some Christian circles this would be seen as the proverbial "too strong." Jane is a person of great conviction, which sometimes means telling a hard truth when it needs to be said. What is persuasive is that finally, Jane Eyre is virtuous (another concept one hears little about) and dignified in the way that Elizabeth Bennet, the heroine of *Pride and Prejudice,* also is, with the difference that Jane's choices are influenced by God's overt action in her life. The foundational premise in these remarks is that it takes spiritedness and conviction and even telling a hard truth to be truly virtuous and dignified, a virtue and dignity that involves purposeful attention to one's mind, one's soul and its longings, and one's spirit, all of which affect one's physical life.

It seems possible to suggest that the average Christian girl and woman may learn more about how to do this from classic novels like those of Jane Austen and Charlotte Brontë than from a Christian women's magazine, a Christian romance novel, a Christian-living book, or from some women's conferences. I can hear some readers saying—can't you find something more current than these books to illustrate your point with contemporary women? The definition of classic is a work that lasts, that is dated only in superficial detail such as particularities of dress and speech, but whose themes are universal and timeless. These novels are specific, hard-hitting, do not resort to pious clichés, and they show consequences. They show instead of just telling, one of the first principles any writing or speech teacher tells her students. They are also elegantly written. And, while profoundly moral (all truth is God's truth), this novel is not "religious," generally or specifically.

Beloved for years by women of every age and class, *Pride and Prejudice* and its various film takes show the contrast between silly women who make poor choices and a heroine who, while flawed, is nevertheless principled, modest, noble, self-disciplined, and digni-fied. Even non-Christian women whose moral code, philosophy of modesty, and dating behavior aren't remotely like those of the novels' characters appear to be engaged. One can only speculate, then, that women yearn for the very dignity and restraint they eschew by allowing themselves to be clones of the culture; they long to be respected and cherished even when they choose men who do neither; they want to be like Elizabeth Bennet and Jane Eyre or at least to end up being loved as these heroines are by good men. Many of them, Christian and non-Christian seem, however, unable to navigate the paths to such conclusions.

Elizabeth Bennet, while having attractive features, is not said to be beautiful. What emerges far more clearly is her wit, her intelligence, her honesty in speaking her mind, her refusal to accept disrespect even from the man she loves, her willingness to be alone rather than compromise her soul, and her independence exercised with restraint. In summary, she is the picture of dignity.

And that is what seldom comes up today, the crucial role that dignity needs to play in the development of every woman who claims to know Jesus Christ as personal Savior. This is what needs to inform every facet of a woman's life, every choice she makes. I'm not even sure *dignity* is a word anyone has thought about for a long time.

WHAT DO YOU THINK?

I have wondered through the years who Christian women's role models are and if they are getting the purposeful guidance they need from older women. I have informally asked groups of young women this question yearly in a class I teach. Depending on the year, three or four names come up. One or two of them is usually the latest well-known female author/speaker of the day; the others are historical figures like Susanna Wesley or Amy Carmichael. Or they name a grandmother, a mother, or a sister, something which usually has more conviction and specificity. The women I ask seem to have a hard time thinking of people or articulating what they are modeling themselves after.

I found interesting what one young woman wrote about Emma Watson, who plays Hermione Granger in the Harry Potter film series. "When a young woman has grown up with millions of people watching her entire adolescent development, criticizing and controlling her physical appearance, and confusing her identity with that of a fictional character, the pressures make consistent dignity seem impossible. Emma Watson has lived this life with dignity and self-respect, prizing her education, maintaining privacy, avoiding scandals, conducting interviews and public statements with grace, and encouraging other women to have self-respect."[6] Whether or not you agree with this assessment, it hits many of the right notes.

So, I ask you to think about the question: What do you think of when you hear the word *dignity*? Perhaps more specifically, who do you think of? What person comes to mind? Is it a popular singer, speaker, movie actress, or perhaps a friend or relative? And how do you picture dignity? Is it something you aspire to be? What would you change about yourself to be dignified?

DIGNITY DEFINED

Dignity: the word, again, deserves a close look. The first or second definitions of the word from a variety of dictionaries are as follows: "formal, grave or noble bearing, conduct or speech; nobility or elevation of character; the quality or condition of being worthy, esteemed or honored; inherent nobility and worth; poise and self-respect; formal reserve or seriousness of manner appearance, or language."

Dignity, it is clear, is not the same thing as poise; it is not the same thing as beauty, and it is certainly not the same thing as style though, of course, a dignified person may have any one or all of those qualities. Probably the characteristic most confused with dignity is poise, defined as "to be balanced or held in equilibrium: balance; freedom from affectation or embarrassment; composure."[7] Little about this definition suggests much about the internal values of the person or about her character; instead, it describes an outward behavior that may or may not be influenced by internal stability and integrity. Many of the celebrities presented to us in media outlets have been poised, although admittedly, even that is becoming a thing of the past as one looks at the embarrassing and ludicrous behavior of so many who are having what Andy Warhol called their fifteen minutes of fame.

The truth of the matter is that most of us are in process, no matter what our age.

Probably one of the most famous individuals in modern history who consistently and deservedly has been called poised is Princess Diana, whose decisions, as she suffered disappointment and betrayal, were deeply flawed and led to undignified choices and the tragedy of her life. Interestingly enough, Mother Teresa, who died within a few days of Princess Diana, was probably seldom described as poised, but always seen as dignified, an issue of character. In recent history, Laura Bush was seen by almost everyone on both sides of the political spectrum as dignified and graceful. These were qualities that emanated from her person; while not beautiful, she was often radiant without being showy; when asked hard, even rude questions by her husband's enemies, she answered with gracious conviction, and sometimes a sense of disarming humor. She handled the duties of the White House without bringing attention to herself; she was modest and contained.

Dignity contains within it, as the definitions suggest, not only noble *bearing*, a facet of appearance, but also noble *character* which comes from *inherent* nobility and worth. That means the person is sure of her values and beliefs, she is sober and thoughtful about every part of her life. And, what this discussion is trying to do is to introduce to you dignity's importance, not to present yet another unreachable ideal. If you can see the crucial role of a quality, it is possible to begin the journey toward that quality because it promises a life of greater integrity. The truth of the matter is that most of us are in process, no matter what our age. It is easier for some of us to look dignified than others, but to truly be dignified is something different that has a number of components.

Just as I have never heard or seen advertised a seminar called "How to become a formidable, self-possessed woman of fully realized moral sensibility," I have also never seen one entitled "How to Be Dignified in Your Choices," though of course wise books and innumerable articles have been written and countless presentations made about making good choices. Oddly enough, given its importance, one seldom hears the word *dignity* discussed as a value for human behavior by non-Christians or Christians although it may be used to describe someone from time to time. If you do a cursory search of articles on dignity, besides random references in Christian blogs here and there, you'll find mostly pieces addressed to the medical and social services communities, articles about helping people to die with dignity and the disenfranchised to find dignity through a better life. John Paul II wrote about the dignity of women in one of his apostolic letters, arguing that Christianity, more than "any other religion" has given women special dignity and urges the church to use them in more significant ways.

Dignity is a strong, chosen, deliberate way of life, the result of the totality of a person's choices and worldview.

When dignity is talked about among Christian women, it most often has to do with the passages about wives' behavior in 1 Timothy and the proverbial "quiet and submissive spirit," a phrase that is seldom correctly scripturally interpreted and is too often equated with passivity contributing to women's voicelessness. Passivity, wrote one clinical psychologist, "is born of anxiety; it is a fear of using our energies lest we risk disapproval by others or risk failure in our own eyes. . . . It is a disowning of our nobler parts—our self-reliance, our courage under fire, our resolve to win, our determination to inspire others to greater heights."[8]

DIGNITY LIVED OUT

To be a Christian woman of dignity, a woman must know who she is before God; she must have dealt thoughtfully with her personhood and made decisions about who she will be. Dignity is a strong, chosen, deliberate way of life, the result of the totality of a person's choices and worldview. Which takes us back to Jane Eyre, who is a model of that kind of living. Again, I chose this book, not because of its age, but because of its unusual central character, one whose strength and character stand out enduringly.

Jane Eyre endures oppression, starvation, madness, condescension, and coldness. She is presented with a number of women role models whom she observes, learns from, and departs from to become her own person. One of those models is too ideal, too compliant, though good. Another is too angelic, and still another sometimes passive-aggressive. Jane is too strong to compromise her convictions, and she is passionate, qualities which presented problems for Victorian critics and perhaps for us today at times. And, she dares to suggest that singleness is preferable to an inappropriate marriage.

If you know the story at all, Jane Eyre is the account of a young, orphaned British girl who goes to live with an aunt and cousins, all of whom treat her cruelly. She is then sent to a boarding school for poor girls, where a supposedly Christian director, actually a monster, treats the orphans abusively and tyrannically—many of them dying of cold-related illnesses and starvation. All of this has historical precedent in the times of the novel and was part of Charlotte Brontë's and her sisters' experience.

Jane, who does not have the advantage of good looks or good fortune, survives in spirit because she chooses the path her life (spirit, mind, and behavior) will take, often against cultural mores and corrupt authoritative voices, She has a sense of voice from the time she is a child and tells the truth in every circumstance, even when it could endanger her well-being. Though she must learn to refine her expression, she will not silence the voice of her intellectual needs or mute her moral voice by compromising her character with poor relational or sexual choices for the sake of fleeting happiness. She rises to a higher standard, a God-given understanding of righteousness.

So, first of all, she tells the truth, a righteous truth. She trusts her instincts—something women are often prone to ignore. She doesn't go along with the conventional wisdom that says "keep quiet, take the abuse, answer questions the way you're expected to." She calls her aunt on her cruel behavior. She refuses to give pious answers to the evil school director, Mr. Brocklehurst, when he asks her supposedly "spiritual questions" about the Bible. Listen to the following exchange—starting with his attempt to intimidate her.

"Do you know where the wicked go after death?"
"They go to hell," was my ready and orthodox answer.
"And what is hell? Can you tell me that?"
"A pit full of fire."
"And should you like to fall into that pit, and to be burning there for ever?"
"No sir."
"What must you do to avoid it?" . . .
"I must keep in good health, and not die." [replies Jane][9]

The reader can't help smiling at this childlike honesty, but also the kind of truthful spirit that will become "a strong moral sensibility." That's the kind of women I think Jesus wants us to be—that's the kind of biological and spiritual daughters He wants us to raise, women who have a righteous instinct for recognizing, naming, and resisting abuse and falsehood.

When Jane leaves the boarding school, she goes to Thornfield, an estate where she becomes a governess for a young girl. The job of governess was only as good as the employer made it. Anything could be done to governesses, and, because of what they endured, the proportion of them in mental asylums was substantial. While Jane is grateful for the job, she is not subservient. She remarks:

> It is in vain to say human beings ought to be satisfied with tranquility; they must have action; and they will make it if they cannot find it. . . .
> Women are supposed to be very calm generally: but women feel just as men feel; they need exercise for their faculties, and a field for their efforts as much as their brothers do; they suffer from too rigid a restraint, too absolute a stagnation, precisely as men would suffer. . . . It is thoughtless to condemn them, or laugh at them, if they seek to do more or learn more than custom has pronounced necessary for their sex.[10]

These words still ring strong today as they were shocking then, 160 years ago, but they show an accurate understanding of the need for women, as human beings, to fulfill their gifts, to use their creativity, to stretch beyond prescribed activities and passivity to true humanity. Dignity requires the development of principle and the use of intelligence.

When Jane meets Rochester, her boss, and the man who becomes the great love of her life, she nevertheless keeps her sense of voice, outrageous then as it is now. At one point, when he has been condescending to her, she says to him articulately to say the least:

> Do you think, because I am poor, obscure, plain, and little, I am soulless and heartless?—You think wrong!—I have as much soul as you,—and full as much heart! . . . It is my spirit that addresses

your spirit; just as if both had passed through the grave, and we stood at God's feet, equal,—as we are![11]

This is not a woman who can be put down or forced into false submission by her social position or the dominance of the man who loves her. Charlotte Brontë was severely criticized for this work because she dared to portray a woman who would not surrender to the worst of her culture's expectations—would not give up her sense of self and conviction, no matter what her social caste. This is a woman who puts a high value on herself as God does also. In her own defense, in the face of critics who accused her of presenting an inappropriate model for young women and who called her sensibility "masculine," Brontë wrote the following words in the preface to the novel's second edition: "Conventionality is not morality. Self-righteousness is not religion. To attack the first is not to assail the last. To pluck the mask from the face of the Pharisee, is not to lift an impious hand to the Crown of Thorns."[12] In other words, what has always been done culturally is not the same as moral principle. Pointing out the hypocrisy of what a person or church has decided is appropriate is not an attack on the person of Jesus Christ.

As I say to my students, Jane and Rochester are not just "in heat."

I wonder how many young women reading this feel that sense of self, that sense of worth before God, a worth that extends to their choices and ability to stand for what they know is right? I wonder how many women in general can make the distinction between what their subculture dictates (the church, the circles they occupy) and true morality, between the self-righteousness of peer pressure and true conviction, between pharisaical demands and what Christ wants His daughters to be?

Not only is Jane truthful and thoughtful, but she is also morally resolute; she does the right thing in the face of great temptation, a righteous behavior which is not accidental but born of a *whole* life filled with the practice of character, what we would call holiness. So, when Jane must leave Rochester, whom she has in her need for love made a god (I will not insert a spoiler for those who have not read the novel) yet with whom she has fallen deeply in love, she runs like Joseph ran from Potiphar's wife. This is no small act, as the love Jane and Rochester feel for each other is completely different from the shallow relationships usually drawn in formulaic Christian or secular romance novels and even in some personal accounts.

In much the same way that Darcy and Elizabeth are attracted to each other in *Pride and Prejudice*, Jane and Rochester are drawn to each other because each finds the other so interesting. Each admires the other's strength and thoughtfulness (by this I mean giving thought to) as shown in behavior and conversation. Each challenges the other in the best sense of the word. This is a connection of the minds which leads to a deeper, more enduring passion than that sparked by a less layered attraction. As I say to my students, Jane and Rochester are not just "in heat." So, Jane's refusing to sin is the result of her moral resolve, her sense of identity before God, her choice of what is right over what the heart wants. Her choice is "spirited." This is the refusal to surrender to desperation or fear of being alone; it shows nobility of character and dignified living.

Listen to the process Jane goes through in the midst of loss, of homelessness, of nothing to quiet her terror but God and in the face of her overpowering love, attraction, and compassion for Rochester. First of all, she asks herself the question any woman who has loved can understand. Think of a time when you have been dating a man who has a pornography problem, who is not treating you well, or who isn't good for you spiritually, emotionally, or physically. Jane feels torn by her beloved's desolation—she wants in our vernacular "to be there for him." She says, "Feeling . . . clamoured wildly. 'Oh, comply!' it said. . . . 'Soothe him; save him; love him; tell him you love him and will be his. Who in the world cares for *you*? or who will be injured by what you do?'" In the wake of her pity, her habit of thinking rationally and theologically and her self-respect kick in. "Still indomitable was the reply—'*I* care for myself. The more solitary, the more friendless, the more unsustained I am, the more I will respect myself. I will keep the law given by God; sanctioned by man.'"[13] *Indomitable* is another of those words that deserves a closer look. It means "incapable of being overcome, subdued, or vanquished."[14] Here, of course, the sense of it is that even the greatest passion, the deepest human longing cannot overcome Jane in the face of truth, of what she knows to be right.

Finally, in one of the more powerful theological statements Jane Eyre makes, she teaches her readers the foundation of how one is to live when she says with desperate determination, "I will hold to the principles received by me when I was sane, and not mad—as I am now. Laws and principles are not for the times when there is no temptation. . . . They have a worth—so I have always believed; and if I cannot believe it now, it is because I am insane—quite insane: with my veins running fire, and my heart beating faster than I can count its throbs."[15] To rephrase, God's laws are easily kept when one is not enduring temptation. How committed we are to what we say we believe is tested when we are "insane," literally out of our minds with temptation, when it is hard to remember truth.

DIGNITY AND MEMORY

Approximately two hundred uses of the word *remember* appear in the Old and New Testaments, many of them reminders to recall the historical events through which the patriarchs passed so that their descendants might be given faith. Readers are urged to remember how God led His children and their enslavement and deliverance, to consider the generations long ago. They are even urged to ask their fathers for that history. Readers are called upon to extol God's words and wonders, to remember the ancient laws and find comfort in them. The failure to remember marks some of the great defeats of the children of Israel. Sometimes my mother used to say to me as I went out with my friends, "Remember who you are and whom you belong to." Dignity demands that we remember that we are daughters of God, that we belong to Him at all times, but particularly when as Jane says, we are "insane."

If your faith matters, your mind matters.

What helps Jane in temptation and loss is both her ability to think critically in a moment of passion and her theology—her objective belief in a God of truth, her insistence upon remembering truth. She understands that she must behave with righteousness and dignity in spite of what she feels. She must live above her emotions as powerful as they may be; she must not rationalize her choices, choices which make all the difference in her life, the difference between wasting time in sin and trusting God for her happiness. And, it makes her a model to others, proof that one can live wisely and well.

If your faith matters, your mind matters. If your mind matters, it is important what you do with it, theologically and intellectually. You cannot separate your spiritual life from the life of the mind. You can't be fully human without using wisely all the faculties God has given you. They are intertwined; one will not thrive without the other. In neglecting one or the other, you will live a small, shriveled existence. Jane makes the right decisions because her intellectual reasoning ability and theological understanding are sound, protecting her from moral failure.

The culture has encouraged so much self-focus and indulgence that sometimes I wonder if we haven't told ourselves we can't be heroines in the old-time tradition. Being a heroine means being countercultural where culture or subculture is wrongheaded. Everywhere we look, people are telling stories of recovery from sin; and, of course, God's grace is marvelous beyond words. However, it is possible to choose well, to spend less time recovering and more time deepening our walk with God.

In J. R. R. Tolkien's *The Hobbit*, the magician Gandalf tells the reluctant and unlikely hero Bilbo Baggins, "There is more to you than you know,"[16] more in this instance than doing what he has always done. The wise magician knows that Bilbo has become addicted to that cozy hobbit hole; he likes eating and drinking well, he likes being comfortable. But Gandalf knows that Bilbo has two sides to his nature, that "within the hobbit's veins coursed blood not only from the sedentary Baggins side of the family but also from the swashbuckling Took side."[17] Bilbo has gotten used to the sedentary side, and after all, he's not doing anything wrong; he's just a nice, even generous, placid hobbit who knows how to have a good time, who fits into his community. But, something transcendent is calling to Bilbo—telling him there is more to life than this, that there are adventures to be had on a heroic scale, that there is good and evil in this world, and he has to be part of fighting the wrongs. Bilbo has a choice at this point, to continue to observe the status quo or to have an adventure which will make him a hero. It is a difference between the status quo as spiritual death, and the transcendent adventure which is life. It's a choice each one of you is being called to make.

DISCUSSION QUESTIONS

1. What is your concept of dignity? How has it changed after reading this chapter?

2. Who do you find dignified and why? Be specific.

3. How do you see dignity as a component of Christianity?

4. Form a book club and read one or both of the novels mentioned in this chapter with a view to forming a philosophy of dignified womanhood.

SUGGESTED READING

• FICTION: *Jane Eyre* by Charlotte Brontë or *Pride and Prejudice* by Jane Austen. Choose unabridged editions.

• NONFICTION: Biographies/autobiographies of women in missionary work; women in Christianity. (See *Biographical Dictionary of Christian Missions*, edited by Gerald H. Anderson.)

CHAPTER 2

FINDING YOUR VOICE
Knowing and Being Known

BY PAM MACRAE

VOICE: The ability to manifest and affirm in
relationships aspects of self that
feel central to one's identity.[1]
The right or opportunity to express
a choice or decision.[2]

Women are supposed to be very calm generally:
but women feel just as men feel; they need exercise for their faculties,
and a field for their efforts as much as their brothers do; they suffer from too
rigid a restraint, too absolute a stagnation, precisely as men would suffer. . . .

It is thoughtless to condemn them, or laugh at them, if they seek to do more
or learn more than custom has pronounced necessary for their sex.[3]

JANE EYRE

It has been thirty years, but I still remember that one of my strongest and most unexpected emotions as a new mother was frustration. I am sure there was never a more enamored mother, like most mothers convinced my daughter was the most remarkable child ever born. My frustration came from being unable to know what she was thinking, feeling, or wanting. I remember looking deeply into her wide eyes thinking, "I just want to know *you.*"

As she began to communicate by smiling, crying, and lisping her first words, I felt the connection that comes with knowing another person. I felt a deep sense of belonging when I finally began to understand what she meant when she cried, reached for something, or when she formed rudimentary sounds, not yet like words but with meaning all the same. I was beginning to know who she was. She also searched my face for information, my response encouraging her to try again. If I didn't understand what she was trying to tell me, she worked at it until her face lit up with satisfaction when she finally got her point across. The connection was mutual. We were beginning to know each other.

VOICE: AN INTRODUCTION

The expression of the essence of one's self, one's thoughts, feelings, and uniqueness, is quintessentially the concept we call voice. When you tell me about yourself, you reveal your identity and personhood. What is uniquely you? And how is that different than who I uniquely am? One's voice is expressed by revealing one's thoughts, but also by one's presence, style, and posture. When we talk and enjoy the presence of another, we are exchanging essences. God created us to be known and models how He knows and wants to be intimately known by us. No one is meant to be alone.

A classic definition of voice refers to the ability to manifest and affirm in relationships aspects of self that feel central to one's identity. Speaking one's feelings and thoughts in relationship is part of creating, maintaining, and recreating one's relational identity. Thus, voice refers more to the *substance* of what is communicated or hidden in relationship than to speech acts themselves.[4]

Voice is not solely offered through one's words, but also through one's presence and a willing engagement of the whole self. The way you nonverbally communicate is part of the expression of your "voice." Walking into a room slowly with your head down and heaving a great sigh tells me something, as does your bouncing into a room and glancing around with glad fervency to find someone to greet. While these are not deep revelations, the actions help to inform me about you.

Relationship happens when we learn to understand the voice of another. Some relationships are close and personal, such as the mother-daughter relationship described earlier. Some are distant. We often imply we "know" people we have never met. Public figures or historical persons reveal their voices through their books, through speeches, blogs, or musical compositions. Each person has a personal voice that communicates identity.

It is interesting to think about why a woman at any stage of her life offers her voice—or what factors compel her to keep it in reserve. Think about the circles of your relationships: your family, friends, teachers, church, and coworkers. Each relationship requires that you show up and engage with other people. Are you comfortable expressing your voice? Do you feel invited to do so? Why one offers her voice also begs the question of what makes her feel welcomed to do so. Sometimes it is easier to identify what stops you in your tracks. You may notice it is you who gives signals to the other person, signals that say "stay back," "don't go there," "don't tell me what I don't want to hear."

Most of what we feel is unexamined and unarticulated. Cultural norms are unwittingly absorbed.

Using one's voice does not mean that full disclosure is the goal of every relationship. Sociologists describe the levels of communication in varying ways to help us understand the progression of intimacy. Typically, the progression begins with a low-level social interaction such as the, "Hi, how are you, have a nice day" stage. At the most intimate stage of communication, we feel a sense of liberty to speak our deepest feelings. The in-between levels include incremental disclosures varying from person to person, moving from revealing personal facts, to general opinions that essentially carry no risk, and finally to meaningful personal convictions. Disclosure may be offered as a way to "test the waters" to see if the other person will meet us at the level to which we move.

One can legitimately disclose one's voice at each level. A brief social greeting to the checker at the grocery store is an opportunity to offer a kindness that shows the dignity and graciousness representing one's voice. The goal is not to have unrestrained disclosure in every relationship, but to know at any level of communication that we are not holding back our true voice out of fear.

Personality is often the first window through which we peer to see into a person, but both extroverts and introverts can use their natural personas to control self-revelation. Some extroverts seem to disclose a lot; in reality they use gregariousness to keep you at bay. Some introverts use their shyness as the comfortable rationalization of their lack of self-revelation.

VOICE INHIBITED

Young children begin very early to internalize information that either encourages or discourages self-disclosure. Cues are intuitively understood. Most of what we feel is unexamined and unarticulated. Cultural norms are unwittingly absorbed. We learn when to speak and when to stay silent. If I had rebuffed my daughter as she worked hard to communicate to me, and if when she searched my face for encouragement and affirmation, I had turned away, she might have learned early that seeking to be known and understood is at best an elusive effort.

Who among us has not heard the common sayings, "Children are to be seen and not heard," or, "If you can't say anything nice don't say anything at all"? While these continue to inform our behavior well into adulthood, Christian women, both young and older, often develop deeper quandaries based on personal reading of and/or hearing the teaching of scriptural passages that seem to say she must be silent and submissive, and that she must deny herself.

Over the past thirty years, I have been involved in ministry to women in the church, and for the past seven years I have been a professor at a Bible college. In that time I have had numerous conversations with women who are sincerely conflicted about how to legitimately bring their voice into relationships simply because of their gender.

Sadly, she was led to question her value as a person more *after* she entered the church than before.

One woman told me she realized it was much easier for her to use her voice when she was single and working in the business world. After she left her job, became a Christian, and began to engage the life of the church, things changed. Now, as she thinks about how the use of her voice changed, she realizes that in Christian circles, she felt all the relational lines had been redrawn to caution her against using her voice. In secular society, her full engagement as a woman was not questioned. Men and women worked together to get a job done and were rewarded for their competence. "I felt a sense of energy when I showed up to a meeting at work where I was prepared to engage collaboratively. When I attend meetings at church, I don't expect to contribute and often feel it would not be my place to do so," she said. The difference she noticed as she entered the room was predominantly internal. In one she felt integral, the other incidental.

Now, however, she feels a box has been drawn for her with four strong walls labeled, "Submission," "Quiet," "Gentle Spirit," and "Authority Structure." Her competence is not always considered. Sadly, she was led to question her value as a person more *after* she entered the church than before. When she inadvertently stepped over invisible lines by asking questions or starting conversations, she felt the message was clear that she had gone far enough. Whereas her salvation gave her confidence in the purpose and value of her life in eternity, on a human relational level, she felt her place at the table was marginalized, her voice kept at bay. In seeking to have godly relationships, she often felt confused by the complicated, subtle messages that she had to be distant, cautious, and not engage too personally to appropriately relate to men.

Notice your own reaction when in a conversation, meeting, or group discussion. Do you easily contribute your best thoughts, ideas or questions, or do you scan the room and assess your place and hold back? It is helpful to ask yourself if you are hiding yourself in the situation. Do you have a sense that it would in some way not be "right" for you to involve yourself? Is the reason proper social protocol (the "don't challenge your boss in public" kind of decorum), or do you question whether your voice has value?

The matter of godly submission with dignity, which means living in preferential deference to the other, does not eliminate one's voice; it should characterize it.

The woman I spoke of earlier said she also was cautioned that to bring her voice to decisions and discussions in her marriage ran the risk of offending her husband's sense of authority as her "head" or threatened his leadership. Her manners, speech, wise timing, or making inappropriate demands were not at issue. She was actually being asked to withhold parts of who she was and what she wanted because to give voice to those things could strain her position as a submissive woman. I asked her, as I have asked scores of women, young and old, what her perception was of the primary biblical teaching on the characteristics of a godly woman. She and so many other women answer the same way by responding, "submission."

Some teaching on marital submission encourages a woman to quiet her voice, ostensibly in an effort to honor her husband. She is to let the Spirit speak to her husband about what is important, not giving voice to her desires. Subtle manipulation is often tacitly approved, albeit with a knowing smile, to encourage a woman how best to get her point across without her husband knowing what was happening. The matter of godly submission with dignity, which means living in preferential deference to the other, does not eliminate one's voice; it should characterize it.

At church, the woman inferred from the leadership that she was to speak only when spoken to. Her attempts to conversationally engage matters of interest to her in the ministry of the church felt undervalued; often, her attempts were ignored completely. She is a highly intuitive and sensitive woman who has great insight into specific needs and relational concerns in the congregation. Those gifts are valued in her home, but not at church. It is a critical loss in the life of the church when the caring, nurturing gifts of women go unused.

She began to realize compulsory steps were required of her in this dance, involving carefully nuancing her remarks, monitoring and measuring her tone, and speaking tentatively, in a hesitant voice so as to not appear "too strong." It wasn't that she had a lot of requests; she merely wanted to be included in some of the conversations. One other woman told me that anytime she even asked a question, she felt church leadership viewed her as dangerous, as if any use of her voice pushed against their view of male authority. She voiced a fear I hear often from Christian women, that of being blackballed. "I have known women who after speaking up were rarely ever asked to do anything again at church. Now I understand more fully why I feel more comfortable asking my husband to voice my thoughts than speaking of them myself." Both she and her husband would agree that when he speaks, he is taken more seriously and is better received, when in reality she is the more gifted, gracious communicator of the two.

More than a few women seem to have a fear that any misstep will mean the lines of available ministry within the church will be drawn even more exclusively so as to push them further to the fringe by not allowing or inviting them into places of ministry or service. It can feel risky on both sides for women to engage fully. Honest conflict hovers around as women wonder if they are giving too much while leadership wonders if they are allowing too much.

Strength seems to be valued when it is an internal, unseen quality, but not so much when paired with a woman's voice. How many Christian girls and women, simply by expressing opinions or entering conversations, have heard this confusing message: "You come across as such a strong woman . . . no, no—I mean that as a compliment, really, I do." As a result, it is possible that being viewed as a strong woman appears to be a spiritual defect. When a woman feels compelled to hold back from revealing her essence, to withhold her voice, one must ask if the reason is fear. Is there more safety in hiding?

VOICE AND RELATIONSHIP

Several years ago, Dana Jack, a psychologist and professor at Fairhaven College at Western Washington University, did an extensive study of women affected by depression. She researched the occurrence of withholding one's voice, or in her term, "self-silencing," in women who suffered from depression. The foundation of her premise was that women, as a group, highly value relational intimacy, so a woman who loses her sense of voice in relationships is likely to experience insecurity, fear, sadness, and anger. These emotions also bring a sense of powerlessness, the front door to hopelessness. Not being able to bring your voice to a relationship means you are not really counted, valued, and cannot possibly be truly cared for.

Jesus knew *her*, not just her reputation.

When our sense of well-being is unstable, we are tempted to focus on our insecurities, often a precursor to certain types of depression. Jack makes a strong connection between self-silencing and depression. Her study widely documents the fact that women suffer from depression twice as much as men.[5] Statistics on Christian women and depression are no different. Jack says, "Self-silencing, therefore, refers to removing critical aspects of self from dialogue for specific relational purposes. How a person uses his or her voice is profoundly affected by the anticipated response from the social context."[6]

This makes good sense to me. If I am in a relationship in which

I am concerned that the response to "bringing myself to the table" will be in any way negative, I am tempted to hold back. I certainly count the cost. I ask myself: Is there potential for me to be scoffed at, to be dismissed, or worse yet, might this incite subtle abuse of any kind? Is the risk worth it? Many women conclude that it's not. It is beyond the scope of this chapter to address the issues faced by women who use their voice and suffer the severe consequences of physical, emotional, or spiritual abuse, but that devastating reality is far too familiar to many of us, young and old.

GOD'S INTENTIONS FOR VOICE

God affirms His intention for us to use our voices and not self-silence when again and again questions are posed to draw out the experience of particular individuals in Scripture. It is *we* who ridiculously try to hide from Him, as if that works. When Hagar was running from Sarai, the angel of the Lord found her and asked her where she was from and where she was going.[7] Those were not geographical questions; they were essential life questions. After he gave her words of instruction, comfort, and hope, she responded by naming Him: "You are the God who sees me."[8] She was known, not hidden. Hagar was invited to speak and give voice to her experience. How encouraging that we are summoned to tell God where we are. I believe He is well pleased when our relationships invite the same. The essence of whom we are is our experience, which when spoken has to come from our voice. Hagar was noticed, drawn out by God, and wonderfully experienced as "seen."

In the account of Jesus eating with the disciples at the home of a Pharisee in Luke 7:36–50, Jesus asked Simon if he "saw" the woman who anointed His feet with her tears and perfume and wiped them with her hair. "Do you see her" means more than just an action related to sight. Jesus knew her reputation; He also knew that reputation was all Simon saw when he pejoratively spotlighted her presence. In contrast, Jesus knew *her*, not just her reputation. Jesus points out her greater identity as a forgiven woman. As a result of the astonished relief she experienced after having been forgiven, she freely raised her voice, even without words, by boldly inserting herself into an otherwise inviolable setting. Her fear was replaced by audacious confidence to lay bare her story when not invited to do so. Jesus affirmed her when He openly acknowledged her. He invited the others to do so as well when He asked Simon to "see" her.

A MODEL: ABIGAIL

One of the loveliest and most fascinating Old Testament women who has helped me think through women bringing their voices to difficult situations is Abigail, a beautiful and wise woman who boldly brought all she was into a dangerous and complex situation. She did this with truth and prophetic courage.

I have many unanswered questions about what happened before verse 2 of 1 Samuel 25. We are not told how long Nabal and Abigail had been married, but we do know it was long enough for her to have figured him out, as had his whole household. His servant described him as someone worthless, whom no one could talk to.[9] The general description of him is that he was surly and mean.[10] His name literally means fool, a sad contrast to Abigail.

Nabal was wealthy, possessing three thousand sheep and a thousand goats. As the story opens, his herds had been grazing in nearby pastures, and it was time for the shearing ritual that included feasting. David, the appointed but not yet crowned king of Israel, had been running from Saul, the crowned yet soon to be dethroned king. David and the six hundred men with him had shared closely the pasture space with Nabal's shepherds and flocks. During this time, David not only treated them kindly but also protected them from any harm.

As the time of feasting grew near, David sent ten men to cordially greet Nabal and ask for provisions for a feast. Because Nabal was wealthy, he easily had more than enough food for David and his men. This was not an unreasonable request for several reasons. First, it was culturally acceptable for locals to extend gracious hospitality, including the provision of food, to transients. Secondly, David had extended kind protection to Nabal's shepherds and flocks, which should have been acknowledged by the return of the favor. Two other reasons are also factors. Possibly David was a distant relative, in which case hospitality was expected. Finally, it is certainly reasonable to assume that Nabal knew David was to be the future king since Abigail mentions that as fact when she eventually converses with David.

Abigail expressed herself directly. Her approach was wise; her speech was forthright.

Even so, Nabal responded like the fool he was and laughed at David's request, mocking and insulting him before ten messengers. Only a fool would openly disrespect a future king. When David heard this report, he was incensed and responded rashly by commanding four hundred of his men to strap on their swords and head out to kill Nabal and every man in his house.

A wise servant went directly to Abigail to tell her what was going on, saying, "Now think it over and see what you can do, because disaster is hanging over our master and his whole household. He is such a wicked man that no one can talk to him."[11] Obviously, Abigail had a history of abating her husband's disasters. Abigail moved into action. She "lost no time" in bringing David a generous feast, doing all she could to ensure an audience with David knowing the lives of her family were at stake.[12] She approached David, bowing down with the dignity and humility befitting the future king.

Is it polite, or even appropriate, to call one's husband a fool? After apologizing for Nabal, that's exactly what Abigail did. She assured David that the way in which Nabal responded to him would never have gotten that far had she known what was going on. She then prophetically reminded David of his calling. She knew he was running from Saul, and she beautifully describes the protection his calling ensures as being "bound securely in the bundle of the living by the Lord your God."[13] That wording is lovely. David is secure because of the call of God on his life to rule over Israel. She then challenges him to live up to that calling and keep away from the staggering burden of needless sin that would surely ensue and setting him up for a guilty conscience, a distraction in his kingship. She reminded him he was to fight the Lord's battle, not vengeful battles.

Abigail expressed herself directly. Her approach was wise; her speech was forthright. She told the truth with moral resolve, while firmly reminding David of his calling. Abigail is a woman worthy of respect, a grand picture of a dignified woman who fully knows and uses her own voice.

And what was David's response? He praised the Lord for her. He blessed her for the good judgment that kept him from bloodshed.

Then, having granted her request, he told her to go home in peace. The ESV translates 1 Samuel 25:35, "I have obeyed your voice, and I have granted your petition." The end of the story recounts how the Lord avenges David. Nabal dies after Abigail tells him what she has done, and David sends his servants to quickly swoop her up to be his wife.

THE CONSEQUENCES OF SELF-SILENCING

How do you feel about telling the truth, and when it's appropriate objectively declaring someone a fool? Often, the warning from Jesus in Matthew 5:22 against calling someone a fool clouds our thinking and makes us assume we are never even to mentally identify someone as a fool. Abigail's statement was actually an honest assessment of Nabal's character. Jesus says we are not to contemptuously vilify another person by judging them worthless and then in anger make an absolute declaration, yet Proverbs is full of plumb lines for both men and women with which to measure foolish character. The difference is an issue of attitude.

Hiding, a form of dishonesty, prevents true community.

Abigail was telling the truth. Remember the line "if you can't say anything nice don't say anything at all"? You are wise to tell the truth when it is necessary. Using your voice to speak truth affirms your insight and courage, one of the godliest things you can do. Jesus told the truth, and we must be like Him. Too often when a woman is encouraged not to have a voice, it means she must silence the truth she knows for fear of another person's reaction. Our voice should be foundationally anchored in our knowledge of God and His truth, the context from which we speak and live.

The voice of a Christian woman is not hers alone; it holds great meaning for those who watch and hear her. Think of Abigail's family, the other guests at the Pharisee's house, Ishmael, and even us, the readers of these stories. Their voices matter to all of us. What confidence they had. What dignity. Who else shows you a similar picture?

One woman, otherwise intelligent and capable, told me, "Theology is hard; my husband can just learn it and tell me what to believe."

Some questions obviously come to mind. You may wonder if the desire to bring your voice to the table is self-elevating. Paul says in Philippians 2:3–4 (NIV), "Do nothing out of selfish ambition or vain conceit, but in humility consider others better than yourselves. Each of you should look not only to your own interests, but also to the interests of others." The goal of using our voice is not just to be noticed, but with humility to gracefully be fully present in relationships. Deferring to another person does not require that we be ignored; allowing that is cowardice. Hiding, a form of dishonesty, prevents true community.

Secondly, what happens when women silence themselves either in their church or other relationships? Some church structures have very few on-ramps to invite the voice of women into conversations that influence the life of the church. Support is often given from passages that speak to women teaching men (1 Timothy 2), or the qualifications of elders (1 Timothy 3). However, in reality, those texts do not imply the elimination of a woman's voice in most if not all of those conversations. The reason for the different ethos in otherwise doctrinally identical churches is because the personality and values emphasized by the leadership permeates everything, establishing congregational core values and relationships. "As the leader goes, so goes the nation" is a common saying that echoes in the church.

If a woman internalizes the message asking her to limit her voice, and she self-silences, everyone is ultimately affected. It is dangerous for anyone to feel she is living on the periphery when engaging issues of theology and of knowing God, as will be discussed in a later chapter. If a woman feels silenced, she is also likely to choose a posture of learned helplessness and dependence. One woman, otherwise intelligent and capable, told me, "Theology is hard; my husband can just learn it and tell me what to believe." What she saw in her church somehow communicated to her that she was not meant to substantively engage in concepts of faith. Women who fall into theological dependency may also tend to be self-conscious and insecure when considering how to use their spiritual gifts, doubting the value of their contribution.

One semester, a student summarized her observations in a classroom discussion by saying, "I think part of the problem for Christian women today is that the world expects way too much from women, and the church expects way too little." When women sense low expectations in their church culture, they may naturally acquiesce and assume restrained involvement is the norm. They may pour their energies into whatever work is offered them, but may sense vague disappointment, if not anger, and thoughts of, "if only they would ask me, I could . . . "

My conversations with Christian women reveal a pervasive lack of vision in knowing how to meaningfully use their voices in the church. It is easy to focus on other pleasures, leisure, the newest exercise solution, and even excessively on family, leaving room for little else. Where do you see Christian women together bring voice to intelligent reading, study, or service? Have you quieted your voice about a dream or desire because you don't think it could ever happen?

A critical connection exists between Dana Jack's study about the self-silencing of women and depression, and women who self-silence at school, church, and in other relationships. Women who adapt themselves in structures and relationships by self-silencing may become discouraged, depressed, and withdrawn, forfeiting their God-intended dignity and the fullness of their persons. This is a great loss.

Jack describes what this looks like. She says, "Self-silencing becomes obvious when women try to change their thoughts and when they tell themselves how they 'ought' to feel. Women take the cognitive actions required to adapt themselves to existing structures for many reasons: the fear of retaliation, the desire to keep relationship, or the lack of models for alternative behaviors."[14]

ASSESSING YOURSELF

To assess yourself, ask yourself these questions. Do you observe relationships where you notice a sense of sadness and depression? Does your ability to be engaged in ministry service leave you feeling distant? Where do you not feel known? Do you feel there is a relationship where you silence yourself?

How do women learn to speak up and use their voice without

fear? We need to grow and get better at bringing our voice to relationships. The benefits are immeasurable. We enlarge each other's lives, providing a way to more deeply be part of each other's joys and more fully experience comfort in our sorrows—not to mention the crucial work of confronting each other's sins.

The efforts we make to offer our voice are seldom comfortable or easy. We bring to our relationships all our human frailties. At our core is the sin that makes it easy to offend and be offended. But by *humbly* offering our voice and graciously accepting the voice of another, we reflect God's pattern of relating. To know God and be known by God helps us understand our capacity to be known to each other.

Let's consider Abigail one more time. The "ought" in her situation meant that she "ought" not to speak out against her husband. She "ought" not approach the future king uninvited. She "ought" not speak up. But she did, and David called her blessed. Abigail is a wonderful model for us.

I used to wonder if the structures and relationships that inhibited a woman's voice were the primary reason she found it difficult to use that voice. Now I think every Christian woman must take courage, presenting her essence by using her voice in the face of resistance—Christ's calling to her. Dorothy Sayers describes Christ's attitude toward women unforgettably. Never, she says, did Christ "nag," "flatter," "coax," "patronize," or make jokes about women. He "took their questions and arguments seriously, . . . never map[ping] out their sphere for them." He simply "had no axe to grind." He "took them as he found them." She movingly summarizes, "Perhaps it is no wonder that the women were first at the Cradle and last at the Cross. They had never known a man like this Man—there never has been such another."[15]

DISCUSSION QUESTIONS

1. The term "self-silencing" used by Dana Jack describes what a woman does in relationships that involve some risk. How have you seen either yourself or another woman "self-silence"?

2. Can you identify what situations and scenarios most tempt you to "self-silence"? Is there a fear you identified that can be answered by encouragement from Scripture?

3. How can Christian women resist the temptation to use their voices for self-promotion and instead use them in a way that honors God? How can you know the difference?

4. Abigail is a great biblical model for women. Can you identify a place of service in your church where you could use your voice?

SUGGESTED READING

*   FICTION: "The Revolt of Mother"—a short story by Mary Wilkins Freeman.

*   NONFICTION: Read 1 Samuel 25 for the full story and draw out additional principles you can learn from Abigail; *Half the Church* by Carolyn Custis-James.

CHAPTER 3

LONGING:
FROM DISPARITY TO DESIRE

BY LINDA HAINES

DISPARATE: Made up of fundamentally different and often incompatible elements.

DESIRE: To long or hope for; exhibit or feel desire for.[1]

For now we see in a mirror dimly, but then face to face. Now I know in part; then I shall know fully, even as I have been fully known.[2]

Who could love the creature in the mirror? She was not winsome; she was not prepossessing or sweet. She was neither beautiful like her godmother, nor serene like Maria, nor ordinary-looking like all the girls here. She was, simply, frightening. She even frightened herself.

I could not be loved, a forlorn little voice said inside her. I cannot be loved.[3]

CASSANDRA GOLDS

SEEING ONESELF

So did young Heloise in this quiet, but pivotal moment find herself practically splitting in two, upon seeing herself for the first time in a mirror. In this memorable young adult novel, *The Museum of Mary Child*, described as part fairy tale, part romance, and part mystery, Heloise, the protagonist, has lived for many years in her godmother's cottage where there are no mirrors at all. There she caught her reflection only rarely, and even then, darkly, in the polished surface of a tabletop, or when passing a dark window on the street. As she unexpectedly confronts her "me" staring back from the mirror at the far end of the dormitory at the orphanage where she now lives, she is suddenly flooded with a sense of terrible alienation. Until this moment, she has been only an "I," one person, but now she is two as she gazes at her reflection. She sees little that's notable about herself, although she can see nothing disfigured in her countenance. "But there was, she realized, something frightening about her, something chilling, uncanny."[4] Shocked, she begins to tremble. "'I—I—' said Heloise. She had a vague sense that she was supposed to be hiding something. At the same time, she felt that nothing very much mattered any more. Her throat swelled and ached. After a moment she whispered listlessly, 'I have never seen myself in a mirror before.'"[5]

Heloise has experienced her first startling encounter with a new understanding of herself; she feels shame and a kind of terror. She grows numb in the moment and feels dead; finally, she feels unlovable. Who could love the creature in the mirror, she asks. Who indeed? How artfully Australian author Cassandra Golds captures in this story such a critical moment in the young girl's life. Heloise is not very old at this juncture; she may just be entering preadolescence. Yet, like many of you reading this, she has already borne many hurts, in this case, the hurt of years of living with a distant and cold godmother, one who is rigid and unable to offer her affection. In seeing herself for the first time, Heloise loses her self-possession, the narrator tells us, for until now she "had not realized how separate a thing one's appearance was from how one felt inside. Her first instinct was to say, *'But that's not me!'* For the face that stared back from the mirror seemed alien indeed."[6]

Perhaps you have felt like Heloise. Someone reflects something back to you that doesn't fit your image of yourself, and suddenly you feel alien and alienated—divided.

Another better-known heroine in literature felt a similar kind of alienation when she also looked long and hard into a mirror in the movie, *Pride and Prejudice* (2005, starring Keira Knightley and Matthew Macfadyen) based on the novel by English author Jane Austen. Earlier in the day, young Elizabeth Bennet has rudely turned down a proposal from the proud and handsome Fitzwilliam

Darcy. Mr. Darcy after all, while having professed how "ardently" he admires and loves Elizabeth, has spoken candidly of his concern about his higher station in life and his "sense of *her* inferiority."[7] Furthermore, Elizabeth has learned recently that Darcy was influential in breaking up the relationship between her sister, Jane, and his friend Bingley, both of whom are attracted to each other. Elizabeth is grieved by this news, and angry.

Self-understanding can be a nasty business.

Trying to be the gentleman Elizabeth earlier accused him of not being, Darcy later brings her a letter, his effort to answer painful questions she has rightfully asked regarding his treatment of family and friends. As she reads the letter—and she reads it over and over—Elizabeth is startled at the reflection of herself mirrored in Darcy's words. Like Heloise, she experiences a "contrariety of emotion" and feelings "scarcely to be defined."[8] Until this moment, she hadn't realized her vanity was leading her down a path of foolish and misguided behavior toward Darcy; she has been blinded by prejudice and lack of self-knowledge. She later admits, "I meant to be uncommonly clever in taking so decided a dislike to him, without any reason. It is such a spur to one's genius, such an opening for wit to have a dislike of that kind."[9] Growing increasingly ashamed of herself, Elizabeth admits, "How despicably have I acted! . . . I, who have prided myself on my discernment!—I, who have valued myself on my abilities! . . . How humiliating is this discovery!—Yet, how just a humiliation! Had I been in love, I could not have been more wretchedly blind. But vanity, not love, has been my folly. . . . Till this moment, I never knew myself."[10]

It is fitting, given the time constraints of film, that the movie of this great work depicts Elizabeth in front of a mirror (no mirror is mentioned in the book), implying in this scene her reflection, self-examination, and finally her revelatory admission. Change almost always begins with revelation, with protests, *But that's not me! Surely that's not me!* Self-understanding can be a nasty business. Probably everyone, at some point in her life, has been frightened by the creature she sees in the mirror and has silently exclaimed, *But that's not me!* Speaking fancifully, is it possible that even Eve, the first woman, caught a glimpse of her dim reflection in the apple she had just picked and polished, and was about to eat from the Tree of Knowledge? Is this why she later hid?

Every young woman desires to feel that sense of wholeness that brings confidence and makes her at home with herself and others.

To feel dignified and self-possessed in such a moment is sometimes impossible. When we hear a recording of our voice sounding too high or too low, too flat or too exuberant, we laugh, feeling the strangeness. "No, it sounds just like you," we're told. Or we see a picture of ourselves contradicting how we think we look, or certainly how we hoped to look. We sigh and maybe smile wryly at someone's nervous compliment. But in moments of serious reflection, suddenly aware of a neglected character flaw or someone else's seeing and commenting on that flaw, inside I experience a deep divide in my sense of self. Sometimes the shock overwhelms me. I feel disparate, that is, confused inside, or full of discord between my thoughts and feelings; I feel divided and exposed.

Standing in front of the mirror, Heloise stumbles on her divided self as does Elizabeth when she *sees* her reflected self in the mirror of Darcy's letter that inadvertently shows how prejudiced and proud she has been. Both young women step back to observe their beings—a very different perspective than just *being*—and the instant exposure is painful. Self-consciousness is almost always uncomfortable because it has the extraordinary ability to lay bare the difference, whether great or small, between who I think I am and who I really am. My *self* is suddenly exposed as out of kilter with my environment so that nothing synchronizes, nothing correlates. *I* don't synchronize, *I* don't correlate; and *I*, like Heloise, am "simply, frightening." To stay too long in such emotional free fall is dangerous for anyone. For the Christian, it can ultimately be defeat. At this juncture, one stands at a crossroads.

DIVIDED I FALL

There may be no subject given more attention—certainly in art, classic literature, and history—than that given to the divided self. After all, what other conflict holds more potential for confusion, pain, and possible regret than living life at odds with my *self* or at odds with *others*; the two go hand in hand. Every young woman desires to feel that sense of wholeness that brings confidence and makes her at home with herself and others. Hard as we try on our own to pull ourselves together, the road is difficult and, without help, we will flounder, perhaps becoming a kind of false self, untrue to ourselves, too masked to find our calling. Or, we may bounce back and forth on our journey, without firm ground for traveling.

Painfully torn in our attempts to be whole, we may even disintegrate into what feels like a state of mental and spiritual madness. To paraphrase an old song: united I can stand, but most certainly, divided I *will* fall.

As Christians, we grow up hearing about our divided selves. Aleksandr Solzhenitsyn once said, "The line separating good and evil passes not through states, nor between political parties either—but right through every human heart."[11] The apostle Paul plainly tells us in Romans 7:18b (NIV) of the war between our two natures. He says of himself, "I have the desire to do what is good, but I cannot carry it out." Later, he says, "When I want to do good, evil is right there with me. For in my inner being I delight in God's law; but I see another law at work in the members of my body, waging war against the law of my mind and making me a prisoner of the law of sin."[12] Paul confirms our struggle between two natures, each pulling its own way. He exclaims: I'm wretched with this tug-of-war—this is exhausting! What kind of a God *is* this, he might have wondered, to allow such miserable dividedness? Isn't there a way to work through the problem reasonably?

H. M. Daleski, professor of English at Hebrew University in Jerusalem, also writes about the divided self in his book *The Divided Heroine*, which explores the issue from the standpoint of female protagonists in selected English novels. In a general discussion of the conflict, he draws on an illustration borrowed from the great philosopher Plato who lived 427 to 347 BC. The illustration is found in Plato's Socratic dialogue *Phaedrus* and shows an equally exhausting battle of natures when Plato describes what happens as a pair of horses and their driver, or charioteer, journey toward a beautiful vision representing the soul's immortality or heaven.[13] Plato describes one of the horses as an unruly steed, one "of a dark color" who repeatedly "plunges and runs away" as though not reined in by the charioteer.[14] The steed finally becomes so unrestrained, he "takes the bit in his teeth and pulls shamelessly,"[15] leaping headlong on the beloved of the vision, dragging the charioteer and the other steed with him.

Plato reasons that either the dark horse gets his way and forces both the charioteer and the white horse, representing *good*, to follow his bidding; "or the charioteer succeeds in reining in 'the wild steed,' covering 'his abusive tongue and jaws with blood,' forcing 'his legs and haunches to the ground,' doing this again and again and again until he is 'tamed and humbled' and follows the charioteer's will."[16] What a powerful illustration of the divided self and of what it takes to subdue the dark horse within.

Daleski also borrows from Paul to further study the dilemma of his heroine's divided natures. Paul's teachings were influential during the time in which these English novelists wrote their stories. Daleski notes that Paul takes the struggle further than others, and argues that he even goes "beyond anything Jesus envisaged."[17] For Paul insists on the *opposition* (my italics) of the two natures and he gives them names, "flesh and spirit." Daleski quotes Paul's words in Galatians 5:17: "For the flesh lusteth against the Spirit, and the Spirit against the flesh: and these are contrary the one to the other." And they that are Christ's must "crucify the flesh."

Paul's thinking becomes too much for the English professor who suggests that what Paul sees as a virtue may actually *cause* self-division, not heal it since it requires negating one-half of the self, thus losing the whole. The opposing forces within could be reconciled, Daleski suggests, with a good charioteer controlling them.

Ironically, while we as Christians *believe* Paul's words, that they are opposite, we often *do* what Daleski suggests, trying to harmonize our divided natures, exactly what our culture encourages. For example, every time a young Christian woman rationalizes that sexual involvement at whatever level is okay because she's "in love," she begins the process of self-division, the split between what she knows to be right (the life of the spirit) and what she wants (the life of the flesh). She succumbs to the oft-cited philosophy that Woody Allen made famous in the line, "The heart wants what the heart wants." The heart, defined this way, has quit listening to the Great Charioteer. The dark horse has begun to take charge.

Can we manage our darkness? Paul tells us it can't happen.

Contrary to what most people, including Daleski above, think, compromise isn't always a good thing. When I teach styles of conflict to my counseling groups at work, I use a simple picture to illustrate this. What if one spouse wants to paint the bedroom blue, the other spouse, yellow, and both are adamant? They finally compromise and paint it green. Of course, neither is happy; each person's preference has been denied as has the gift of sacrifice. In time, too many rooms of "compromised" colors might also begin to compromise the marriage. Moving beyond this story to the larger issue, how can one compromise the darkness of one's fallen nature with the lightness of God's Spirit? The mixture can only be grey.

Two individual horses might pull together under a commanding driver, providing a fairly smooth ride—as horse rides go—whether pulling a chariot, a sleigh, or me. And a well-trained driver might get *frighteningly* close to pure harmony if she handles the animals delicately. Frighteningly, I say, because all could be lost trying to maintain such a precarious balance. One slip of the rein, and I make an uncalculated mistake. Two slips, and I begin losing control. Another, and my initial divided self begins to tear further apart, lying finally in a heap bearing little resemblance to a self at all. Can we truly reconcile our delicate dual being? Can we manage our darkness? Paul tells us it can't happen. One or the other nature will prevail; and whichever does makes all the difference in the world.

THE FIRST PRIORITY

If we are to become whole people, women of dignity and self-possession, we must find our way out of the half-lives we may be trying to pass off as whole. We are called to be wise about ourselves and others, to live and choose wisely. Wisdom is a choice, like everything else. And while an old proverb tells us that "wisdom comes with age," God intends us to start searching while we're still young. Heloise, in *The Museum of Mary Child*, was quite young in the story when she first felt shame at seeing her divided self. So was Elizabeth Bennet when she stared into the "mirror" in *Pride and Prejudice*. Scriptural stories, full of the trials and triumphs of their central characters, include persons of all ages, many of them young: Esther, when she was asked by her cousin if she was willing to risk going before the king without invitation to save the Israelites, an act that could have meant lawful death for her; Mary, when she bore the Son of God and "pondered these things in her heart," reflecting with serenity on this marvelous trust, and bearing with dignity her critics regarding Christ's "fatherless" birth. These young girls and others refused to be divided; they wisely chose a better way.

Wisdom calls to every woman who desires it. Solomon states in Proverbs 1:4 that one of his reasons for writing the book is to "give prudence to the simple, knowledge and discretion to the youth." That's a good word to pause over, *discretion*, defined as the "quality of being discreet" which is "having or showing discernment or good judgment in conduct and especially in speech."[18] To be discreet is to be able to distinguish between values, something quite helpful when responsible decisions must be made. Discretion is essential in aiding us to make better choices in every area of our lives, some of the specifics this book addresses. Discretion leads to self-respect and being respected—it is a chosen kind of voice, a core part of dignity. Finally, because it is a godly quality, it leads to the security of knowing our lives are integrated, the fulfillment of what God intends us to be, undivided.

When I look around and see all the reasons women remain divided, starting with the emotional injuries many bring to young adulthood; when I see that older women have often failed to give younger women wise guidance perhaps because they were not guided; when I see the complex and omnipresent temptations and distractions available, some more obvious than others, some subtle and part of the texture of everyday life, I do wonder, what *would* lure young women to spiritual growth, the kind of growth that requires their willingness to look long and hard at the darker side of themselves? There is so much to distract today, unlike the time in which Elizabeth Bennet and Heloise lived, so many more masks to wear. What makes women in the prime of their youth want anything as metaphysical and intangible as godly wisdom and nobleness of character? Or ultimately, what makes them want God?

I guess a few quick answers come to mind, such as Christian

upbringing or your having been discipled by a good Christian friend. Many of you may have been *taught* these values and urged to follow them at some point. Whatever the case, if you are a Christian, the Holy Spirit, after all, is there, wooing you to such desires. But is He? Or is He perhaps losing His heat and warmth in you, His voice suffocated under the weight of your split self? Maybe this higher plane of living feels a little too airy to you, or a little unexciting? Maybe you'd rather have the drama of trying to manage two spirited steeds. Or maybe you'd rather escape your dividedness than face the costly process of confronting your deep-seated longing for wholeness. As well-known writer Larry Crabb puts it, "So much in our everyday living is designed to disguise the horror of living apart from God."[19]

In his book *Inside Out*, Crabb also speaks of the ache in our souls that doesn't go away and calls us to a new awareness of our deep spiritual thirst, an ache that can't "be ignored, disguised, mislabeled, or submerged by a torrent of activity," one that "will not disappear," he writes, because "we were designed to enjoy a better world than this."[20] Writing about our longings, earthly and heavenly, Crabb illustrates them with three circles arranged concentrically. In the outer circle lie our *casual longings*, those things we desire ranging from trivial to more significant. Eating at your favorite restaurant would be a casual longing or, more important, wanting to get into a certain school program. You may feel disappointed when you don't get what you want, but you'll eventually get over it. "We spend our days most clearly aware of our least important longings," the author suggests, "and, as a result, [we] are concerned more with their satisfaction than with the others."[21]

Our *critical longings*, represented by the concentric circle closer to the center, are those involving relationship. Every human, every woman, desires to be loved and respected by others, to see her children lead productive, happy lives, and to find loyal friends whom she can count on for mutual trust and support. These, Crabb states, are examples of our critical desires, which "add immeasurably to the enjoyment of living."

Come back, where are you, you hear yourself wondering. *What are you,* you keep asking yourself.

Finally, at the center of Crabb's concentric circles, are the most important longings that "must be met if life is to be worth living," our *crucial longings*. These are at the core of our souls, residing in our "innermost being," our "belly," as some Bible versions read, our appetite, another meaning of the word. These desires can be met only by God. Crabb concludes, "Nothing can fill that hollow core except what we were built to experience."[22]

GOD'S WILD LOVE

What we were built to experience is God's wild love. Have you ever walked out on a late April afternoon or early May morning and been suddenly startled by a feeling coming over you? You notice a different sense about the air, a certain light in the sky and sun, and a pleasantly familiar breeze? Oh wow, you muse, this feels like spring is coming. And perhaps as you go about doing the things on your mental to-do list, each time you step out of the grocery store, the dry cleaners, or the library, into that scent, that new light, you notice a stirring inside, something that feels mildly unsettling. You're unsure of what's happening; it can feel confusing, but feels hopeful, as well, which confuses you even more. Your stimulated senses play a kind of game of hide-and-seek with your head all day—"Here I am," "No, I'm over here," and sometimes, "I'm hiding now." *Come back, where are you,* you hear yourself wondering. *What are you,* you keep asking yourself.

I don't remember when I first felt what I initially called a "strange feeling" deep inside, that fleeting ache. Looking back, it may have started with John T. McCutcheon's poignant 1912 cartoon illustration called "Injun Summer" (rebranded "Native Indian Summer") which now hangs in the Chicago History Museum and was for years reprinted in local newspapers in the autumn. In it a little boy's "granddaddy" helps him *see* through a field of corn shocks and autumn haze to a long ago world of Indians and teepees and "campfires a-burnin . . . an' th' Injuns are hoppin' 'round 'em." The cartoon misses nothing of the sensual feast of fall, describing its bright red leaves "rustlin' an' whisperin'," its moon hanging over the hill, and "that smoky sort o' smell in the air."[23]

The illustration reminded me of being at my grandparents' when I was young, and of my cousin Barbara. When she came with her family to visit, we'd dash off after lunch to play "Indians" in the big woods not far from the house. We loved Indian lore. A big tree on the only high embankment of a small creek running through the woods was the headquarters where we conducted our important transactions —becoming blood "sisters," burying small toys in a hollow of the tree, and hiding notes to store until some future day when we would retrieve them and recall the "old days," the heyday of our youth.

In time, I came to call my "strange feeling" *sweet sorrow* because it held both sensations, a sweetness and sorrowfulness, the reason for its strangeness, I guess. I liked the peaceful feeling of it and wanted to hold on to it, but it always left quickly. For a while, at least, I thought the feeling was mine alone until I was in graduate school. A professor in a course on psychology and religion began describing his experience of feeling what he called "bittersweet," a description that sounded very like mine. I was thrilled that someone else was confirming my own *sweet sorrow*.

Reading C. S. Lewis's *Surprised by Joy* finally opened my limited understanding of the experience—as it has for many—especially as he wrote of his own "stabs of Joy," also a "kind of unhappiness or grief,"[24] but a grief that we want, one that once tasted, wouldn't be exchanged for all the pleasures in the world. Lewis didn't speak of our longings in the plural as Crabb does in his illustration of the levels of longings. Lewis writes of our longing and desire in the singular, describing them as an inherent state of being that surprises us with sudden swelling sensations—a kind of visitation which teases and baits us toward something or someone very much wanted, but not yet given. He called it the "unsatisfied desire which is itself more desirable than any other satisfaction."[25] It is so delicious, he says, that his experience of it became the central story of his life.

THE IMITATOR

Yet, Lewis also warns us that if we are inexperienced in this mysterious feeling—"and inattention leaves some inexperienced all their lives" he adds—we might think that we know what we long for and mistakenly project the desire onto any number of events, people, or stories of our own that will lead us down the wrong path. One of these is remembering a past, memorable event, longing to return there. Or remembering a previous love and pining for him now. These projections are delusions, for to actually have any of it again would prove inadequate to this strange desire that haunts us. We would not be satisfied. "For I have myself been deluded by every one of these false answers in turn," Lewis admits, "and have contemplated each of them earnestly enough to discover the cheat."[26]

A powerful American short story by Sherwood Anderson, called "Adventure," vividly illustrates delusion led by longing. When a young woman, Alice, begins dating a young man, Ned, all her dreams revolve around him; believing they will always be together, she surrenders to passion. In the heat of the moment and taken with her devotion, Ned says, "Now we will have to stick to each other, whatever happens." Shortly after, Ned moves away, at first faithfully writing, but soon meets someone else and forgets Alice. Clinging to his parting words, Alice feeds her illusory longing, becoming obsessed, for years living only for his return, her personality growing twisted. Finally, realizing he is gone for good, she sees that the great cry of her life was to be loved, in her words to "avoid being alone." She never fully recovers.[27] Because many of us understand Alice, it is chilling to watch the consequences of her insistence upon an illusion. She wastes her life, becoming a caricature, what Anderson calls a "grotesque."

Like Lewis, another writer warns us about being cheated out of the Desire of desires by getting sidetracked by "less-wild lovers," lovers that don't care about integrity and dignity, or about genuine freedom and adventure. These lovers further divide us from ourselves, twisting us, as Alice's misplaced longing deformed her. Brent Curtis, in his striking article "Less-Wild Lovers: Standing at the Crossroads," invites us to experience the most Sacred Romance ever by paying close attention and having the courage to listen, to talk, to even quarrel with the hero of this, what-could-be very wild adventure. "Someone or something," he writes, "has romanced us from the beginning . . . telling us of something—or someone—leaving, with a promise to return." It is a true Romance "couched in mystery and set deeply within us. . . . The longing and desire for it will not go away," he adds, ". . . in spite of our efforts over the years to anesthetize or ignore its song, or attach it to a single person or endeavor."[28]

While the Romance comes and goes at will, surprising us, almost taunting us—similar to Lewis's "stab of Joy"—we might get another unexpected visitor, the author tells us, "another message that comes to all of us in varying shades and intensities, even in our early years." For the Romance has an enemy, one whose message is "dark, powerful, and full of dread."[29] This dreaded message can come through pain and disappointment, through broken relationships or sickness. It can arrive on the back of past trauma suffered from neglect or abuse; or through a long, hard battle with an addiction. Whatever your hurt, anger, or numbness, known or unknown, it will distract you from the sacred and pure desire you once felt. You may even lose your way and yourself. But here you are again, at this crossroads, wondering which direction to take, which message to heed. Because often, when the one message arrives, the other comes just as quickly, and the struggle of our divided self is revisited, this time, more powerfully.

Now more than ever we need discernment and discretion; without these, we are dangerously close to venturing down the wrong path and straying far from the place of integration and peace like two parallel lines that begin closely aligned, but once thrown off even slightly, grow further and further apart until the distance between them is insurmountable.

Less-wild lovers wear many disguises and come in many forms.

Encouraging the divided self, some of you will turn to the less-wild lovers of indulgence to avoid discontent and that deep ache—addictions of all kinds from secret lives of eating disorders, sex, and pornography to shopping. But, there are more, as Curtis points out, some of them even seemingly good, and approved by everyone. "Christian" disciplines also can serve as masks to numb our pain and our longings, or at least, to dumb them down. Trying to be a perfect student, a perfect homemaker, over-busyness at church doing discipleship programs, Bible memory systems, learning witnessing strategies— these duties can become escapes and distractions from noticing what is missing in our souls. "Good things to do," the author agrees, "but the energy to pursue them is often supplied by the expectation that I'll find water that will end all thirst."[30] But thirsty we remain.

In these circumstances, we may eventually find ourselves let down and susceptible to a new spiritual slackness that is fertile ground for a growing curiosity about the Enemy's offerings of subtle and not-so-subtle temptations. At the crossroads where such close facsimiles wait to fool us, we must be careful. We must not get our messages confused, or our messengers, for one of them will only be satisfied when we're not happy. The enemy of the Sacred Romance is manipulative. On the coattail of every virtue we wear gracefully, he hides in a tiny snagged thread, waiting to unravel and steal what is good. The unraveling soon leaves us scarcely covered under a threadbare cloth, until we are exposed with no covering at all, standing naked and afraid.

THE DIVINE PURSUER
All of these escapes and pursuits will certainly lead to self-division if done to numb our longings. They are less wild than the adventure-some Lover we were made for, who, Curtis reminds us, continually

invites us—as He did Israel—into a lovers' quarrel, wanting to make peace and be with us. He calls to us on a new spring day, or on a tawny autumn afternoon with a voice so sorrowful, so sweet, that everything hushes, only briefly, until the wind rises and the leaves start dancing as He sweeps us off our feet. Is that alluring enough, I wonder again, for a young woman to be willing to give up her pitiful lovers and to hope?

In a poem called "The Hound of Heaven," the English poet Francis Thompson (1859–1907), for many years addicted to opium, expresses movingly God's pursuing love of those who have chosen that less-wild lover. Here are a few lines.

> I fled Him, down the nights and down the days;
> I fled Him, down the arches of the years;
> I fled Him, down the labyrinthine ways
> Of my own mind; and in the mist of tears
> I hid from Him, and under running laughter.
> Up vistaed hopes, I sped;
> And shot, precipitated,
> Adown Titanic glooms of chasmed fears,
> From those strong Feet that followed, followed after.
> But with unhurrying chase,
> And unperturbed pace,
> Deliberate speed, majestic instancy,
> They beat—and a Voice beat
> More instant than the Feet—
> "All things betray thee, who betrayest Me."[31]

That is the pursuing love He has for you.

DISCUSSION QUESTIONS

1. How do you see yourself as divided?

2. Where did your division begin? Trace in journal form that story.

3. What experiences of sweet sorrow have you had, from child-hood on?

4. What less-wild lovers have you chosen to numb your longing?

5. What do you see as the spiritual origin of your human longing? How could you nurture this?

SUGGESTED READING

- FICTION: *Till We Have Faces* by C. S. Lewis.

- NONFICTION: *The Weight of Glory* by C. S. Lewis.

CHAPTER 4

"EVERYTHING IS THEOLOGICAL"[1]

BY ROSALIE DE ROSSET

THEOLOGY: 1. The study of the nature of God
and religious truth; rational inquiry into religious
questions, esp. those posed by an organized
religious community. 2. An organized, often
formalized body of opinions concerning
God and man's relationship to God.[2]

Christ in His Divine innocence, said to the Woman of Samaria, "Ye worship
ye know not what" being apparently under the impression that it might be
desirable, on the whole, to know what one was worshipping. He thus showed
Himself sadly out of touch with the twentieth-century mind, for the cry today
is "Away with the tedious complexities of dogma—let us have the simple
spirit of worship; just worship, no matter of what!" The only drawback to this
demand for a generalized and undirected worship is the practical difficulty of
arousing any sort of enthusiasm for the worship of nothing in particular.[3]

DOROTHY SAYERS

What Yentl wants more than anything else is to study the Talmud. "Yentl," a story by Isaac Bashevis Singer, takes place in
Poland in the early twentieth century. Raised in a Jewish community
by her scholarly father, she has secretly been learning the Talmud under his direction in spite of Jewish law which prohibited women from
such a pursuit. In the 1983 movie, based on the story, the following
exchange takes place. Yentl asks her father, "If we don't have to hide
my studying from God, then why from the neighbors?" Yentl's father
answers, "Why? Because I trust God will understand. I'm not so sure
about the neighbors." When her father dies, rather than abandoning
the world of knowledge she so loves, Yentl disguises herself as a boy
and travels to another town, where she joins a Yeshiva, a school for
Talmud study. She is desperate for the knowledge of God.

USING YOUR INTELLECT

If your faith matters, your mind matters; your intellect must be
developed. *Intellect* and *theology* are words that people, and more
specifically many girls and women, back away from. They sound

intimidating; they seem to indicate a superior mentality the average person can never achieve. But the word *intellect* means "the ability to learn and reason as distinguished from the ability to feel or will: the capacity for knowledge and understanding." The second definition is equally enlightening: "the ability to think abstractly or profoundly." Isn't this basic? As Mortimer Adler put it, "One ought to make good use of one's intellect in order to live a morally good life."[4]

What are the alternatives to your using your intellect? To be run by feeling, to ignore your capacity for thinking and acquiring knowledge? To be shallow or unable to deal with profound concepts? Given this definition, doesn't it follow that to be truly human, you *must* develop intellectually as well as emotionally; you *must* reason as well as feel? If so, the question has to be asked: What kind of thinker are you purposing to be, and if you aren't pondering the issue at all, who are you becoming by default? Once again, this is a spiritual life-and-death issue.

What are the alternatives to your using your intellect? To be run by feeling, to ignore your capacity for thinking and acquiring knowledge?

In the story of the woman of Samaria, Christ urges her to know what/whom she worships. She has been living a sad, foolish, promiscuous life, moving from husband to husband, rejected by her community, drinking symbolically from polluted water. To change, she must come to *know* her focus of devotion, past, present, and future. In feeling known by and knowing Christ, her transformation is dramatic.

If theology means knowledge of God, every woman, serious about her faith, young or old, must be a theologian, must move beyond that "simple spirit of worship" to the "complexities of dogma," dogma being the principles and beliefs forming the core of biblical faith, the only reliable guides for life. It is not enough to fit into the life of the church, to be an ethical Christian, to practice generosity to others, and even take part in the service of worship actively. It is not enough to work in an orphanage abroad because of a passion for social justice. It is not even enough to have a disciplined devotional life. In fact, it is possible to be a disciplined Christian, if by that you mean habitual, without being a thinking Christian which means looking carefully, critically (analytically) at all that you hear, read, and do, both in the wider culture and in the Christian subculture. To begin being a thinking Christian is urgent, and the younger you are, the better it is for the way you will live your life. It's like having the best identity protection you can buy. It means taking yourself seriously—as God has all along.

THE INVISIBLE PREJUDICE

The truth is, women who take themselves seriously must overcome cultural handicaps, which takes courage and determination. What women fight regularly is what Shirley Chisholm, the first black woman elected to Congress, called the "invisible prejudice." In an article entitled, "I'd Rather Be Black Than Female," Chisholm argues that being black seems at times less of a handicap than being female. Few people, she reasons, realize how much prejudice actually exists against women while America has been deliberately sensitized to prejudice against blacks for years. Yes, racism is still a problem, but, she says, it is no longer an "invisible prejudice." She writes,

"That there is prejudice against women is an idea that still strikes nearly all men—and, I am afraid, most women—as bizarre." She adds, "Women in America are much more brainwashed and content with their roles as second-class citizens than blacks ever were."[5] So women often suffer at the hands of men and of other women, both groups affected by the invisible prejudice, having been conditioned to live with a subtle or overt disrespect and neglect from men and other women and for themselves that they do not recognize.

Women's invisibility is an age-old problem.

While some things have changed since Chisholm wrote her article in the seventies, and American women have achieved more status and are more protected from discrimination by legislation, the problem is far from solved. Furthermore, the conservative church, maybe intimidated by the worst of the feminist movement's ideology, is running sadly behind, not giving the matter of women's significance in the church enough attention. It is the church above all other institutions that should model the habit of giving worth and dignity to every individual, believing as Scripture teaches that each person is a valued creation of God.[6] This neglect, ranging from active to passive, does not prepare women to take themselves seriously.

Women's invisibility is an age-old problem. In a 1909 issue of *The Institute Tie*, an early Moody Bible Institute publication, columnist Ellen Foster addresses a "complaint" to leaders in the church. Her complaint is that they are "inclined as a rule to emphasize that which is petty and small in woman's life and duties and not . . . as much that which is broad, wide and inspiring." Male leadership overemphasizes, she continues, the femininity of women rather than their humanity, needing instead "to try more to lift woman to a comprehensive thought in Jesus Christ," more crucial than exhorting women to be true to their homes. The implication is that how we live and what we do will follow from a knowledge-driven, biblically based commitment to Christ.[7]

"I have realized that perhaps I have been living and acting based on what I assumed others expected."

Here, Foster points out a serious mistake in the treatment of women, the emphasizing of their gender over their humanity. Dorothy Sayers, writing twenty years later, made the seldom-heard point when she said, "As we cannot afford to squander our natural resources of minerals, food, and beauty, so we cannot afford to discard any human resources of brains, skills, and initiative, even though it is women who possess them. . . . A woman is just as much an ordinary human being as a man, with the same individual preferences, and with just as much right to the tastes and preferences of an individual." Women don't want, she concludes to be "reckoned always as a member of a class and not as an individual person."[8] But, we have often been conditioned to see ourselves first as women and only, at times, incidentally as human beings. Women are first of all human.

RISING ABOVE THE TRANSITORY
Our lives must rise above the "small and transitory," Foster urges, to "study of all things the higher Christian life . . . to talk of the things

of God as well as of the color of their children's eyes and of recipes."
For young, unmarried women, "the color of . . . children's eyes and
of recipes" may translate in its most superficial expression to what's
in style at the latest trendy store; the current practice in shining,
straightening, or streaking hair; or to the ever-present anxiety over
finding a relationship. Foster concludes that it is "soul-nurture"
women need to be engaged in.[9] This is exactly what Christ seems to
have modeled for women so powerfully throughout His ministry
on earth, both in the way He treated them and in the way He spoke
to them. Writing soon after she left college, Dorothy Sayers told a
friend, "I do honestly believe that clear thinking is necessary to the
right kind of faith."[10]

> In addition to the church's widespread neglect
> of women's minds, many women's ministries,
> seminars, and conferences for all ages are not
> filling the gap.

Foster's words a hundred years ago still ring. "Soul nurture" must
be the focus, for " in the soul," writes an Old Testament theologian,
"lies the individuality—in the case of man, his personality, his self,
his ego,"[11] the thing that makes us, what makes us different from
others. The soul composes who we are, and includes our thinking
capacities. Being a thinking person does not happen by accident.
It is a deliberate choice. Passivity, unconscious, even helpless as it
may be, is dangerous; it is a choice of its own kind, and we will not
escape the consequences of mental lethargy.

For many women, soul-nurture of this kind, the way to dignity and a thinking life is something girls and women may have rarely heard presented as necessary; worse yet, it may not have been a significant option. Over and over the young women I teach and spend time with report to me that they haven't heard women's calling talked about "in a way," wrote one student, "that wasn't silly or failed to leave me intellectually valued." Another said, "I have realized that perhaps I have been living and acting based on what I assumed others expected." And one young woman expressed a new awareness of the way theological knowledge can deepen life; it gave her the "satisfaction of drinking deeply from the well of knowledge and the sort of ecstasy that comes from learning something profoundly new." In fact, for her "it was *healing*. Truth can heal. The Lord used the truth about my humanity and personhood, as well as the strength of other women, to remind me of who I was as a created being in His eyes and to remove shame."[12]

THE WEAKNESS OF PRESENT TEACHING

In addition to the church's widespread neglect of women's minds, many women's ministries, seminars, and conferences for all ages are not filling the gap. In fact, with the best intentions, unknowingly, they are perpetuating the problem with weak, experience-based, and superficial biblical teaching that does not speak dimensionally to contemporary needs. As a result, young women go without the foundation needed to counter the seductive pull of their culture; they do not learn discernment; they are not alert to the choices central to their lives as Christians. Alice Mathews, for years Distinguished Associate Professor of Educational Ministries and Women's Ministries at Gordon-Conwell Theological Seminary, is right when she says, "Many women hunger for the Word of God made accessible in a manner that speaks to their situations" which makes the "acute shallowness" of many women's ministries, a tragic reality. Mathews also reveals that women complain of the shallowness of "the Word spoken from the pulpit."[13] Shallow teaching leads to women becoming absorbed with the "small and transitory." To be shallow, ultimately, is to be boring, "and this," writes Sayers, "in the Name of One who assuredly never bored a soul in those thirty-three years during which He passed through the world like a flame."[14]

I have seen the truth of these assertions in specific ways in the years I have been speaking for women's conferences, seminars, and retreats. I agree with Mathews that women are hungry. After all, it is women who plan, lead, and attend so many conferences and Bible studies, who read the greater number of the Christian books on the market; and to whom many of those are written. I have never doubted that the leadership of most women's ministries, national and local, is sincere and well intentioned. However, while there are notable exceptions, too much of what goes on at these events or in church venues is feeling centered rather than content rich, the challenges presented predictable if not downright clichéd. The book tables, with few exceptions, feature a litter of recent Christian how-to or Christian living books on all the conventional subjects publishers think women want to read about or novels in the popular romantic genre, wishful-thinking stories, a subject that will be discussed later. While a number of books are valuable, few of them are Christian devotional or theological classics, not to mention great novels.

More disturbing is how little biblical exposition speakers give, how much they rely on personal stories, how superficial, incomplete, or even inaccurate they can be. For example, I have often done seminars on the importance of reading well to one's life, faith, and witness and also seminars on how to teach a biblical passage responsibly with correct interpretation and theology. Sometimes, when I am contacted, I am asked for topics, and when I explain the details, the person responsible for the retreat or conference is clearly uncomfortable with the subjects, finds them "too heavy," couldn't I do something "lighter" or more user friendly. Or, the contact person may appreciate what I do, but she understands that we will have to work to title the talk or seminar cleverly so as to make it "a draw" which usually means coming up with an "engaging" title, one that may even misrepresent the seminar. The underlying presupposition is that theological, intellectual, or in-depth biblical subjects are not appealing to women, a reflection finally on those who lead the groups, who sadly, have also been underexposed to dynamic, biblical teaching.

And, it's only too true that conditioned as they are, women in general are far more prone to choose the usual potpourri of seminars on how to have a better prayer life, how to do devotions, how to have peace in the midst of hardship, how to do outreach to one's friends and neighbors, how to raise children, how to reach out to a difficult husband, etc. etc., more often than anything that is philosophical, that forms the foundation of all the how-to material which while good, is incomplete.

THEOLOGY IS A COMFORT

That theological study for many women seems boring, or worse yet, threatening is what Carolyn Custis James addresses in her fine book *When Life and Beliefs Collide: Not Knowing God Makes a Difference.* "Survey any group of Christian women on their favorite topics, and theology, if even mentioned, will rank near the bottom of the list. . . . In my ministry to women, I encounter a wide spectrum of negative attitudes toward theology, from indifference to hostility. A few women here and there may find theology fascinating, may even devote a lot of time to study it, but they are exceptional and, in the opinion of some, a little peculiar."[15] Yet, a large number of women who come to my seminars and those like it have thanked me and other speakers for being more theological, biblical, and literary. Other women, exhausted with the usual fare, have been relieved to find something different.

Theology is a word we have associated with scholars, professors, pastors, and men, probably in that order.

These responses and others bear out Mathews's observation about the shallowness of teaching to women. The following words are from young college women, most of them in a homiletics class in which they learn how to exposit the text of Scripture and write a sermon. Writes one, "Generally I shy away from women's retreats, and women's books, and all that type of thing, assuming it will be all the same." Then she began to realize that "women don't have to cop out for the same sappy way it has always been done." "I did not expect to absolutely love the process of studying and preparing for a sermon," says another, "and I had never been so motivated to delve so deeply into a passage, and now that I have, I have grown in my thankfulness for the richness of God's Word. It really is living and active." Finally, and how sad that so many women, young and old, do not realize this—another wrote in her final paper, "Women, I am learning, are deeply purposeful in God's economy. Weak, superficial, teaching and sentimental devotionals will never help young women to see their place in God's work as crucial to His work." Sayers, in her inimitable and brutal analysis, summarizes the problem. She writes, "Let us, in Heaven's name, drag out the Divine Drama from under the dreadful accumulation of slipshod thinking and trashy sentiment heaped upon it, and set it on an open stage to startle the world into some sort of vigorous reaction."[16]

I have read dozens, perhaps hundreds of written essays saying much the same thing. Mathews articulates the remedy: "If we are faithful to our calling, we must do more than merely buttress secular insights with some verses from the Bible. We must build strong biblical foundations so that women (and men) have the tools to deal with daily life. This means that when we open the Word of God to any audience, we must work from the text." That demands informed Bible study, not just talking from a handful of verses or making casual references to a Bible verse as one sees done so often, the Bible lost in the speaker's dramatic personal experiences or group Bible studies based on opinion instead of research, often embarrassing oversimplifications.

We must, as Mathews puts it, "wrestle with the implications of the text within its context." Only then can we apply that text carefully to our lives or teach others to apply it with the consequence, she concludes, that women's hunger will be fed.[17] Being dignified in Bible study means knowing who and what we worship. And, people in general, but women in particular, have had too little opportunity or encouragement to understand their faith and the God they worship in these concrete ways. Then, of course, in the inevitable hard times, there is little in that faith but sentimental ideas and feelings.

Theology, in summary, is a word we have associated with scholars, professors, pastors, and men, probably in that order. Instead, it is our foundation. And, again, it is practical. In my first semester of seminary, coming out of a hard time of life, I took a course in Sin and Salvation under a prominent theologian. That course changed my life. Or, should I say, God, through that teacher's vision, changed my life. I read nearly every one of the nine texts twice and missed only one class though I had to drive many miles four times a week through a hard winter. What I remember most is not a theological outline. What I remember is the aura, the atmosphere of the class. What I can also remember is the longing for God the content filled me with, a longing spoken of in this book, not to be confused with nostalgia or romantic feelings or intellectual stimulation alone, a longing which makes the demands of Christian living not only worthwhile but necessary. The professor made sin concrete. Then, grace became a living thing. I knew who I was, past and present. Custis-James, having had much the same experience, says, "Since theology is really about knowing God, then anyone who believes anything about God is a theologian of sorts." Every woman, young or old, is making theological choices throughout her life.[18]

BIBLICAL WOMEN AS THEOLOGIANS

Many examples could be cited to demonstrate Jesus' regard for women, but particularly interesting are the passages that include Mary, the sister of Martha and Lazarus. While the narrative is familiar, it bears repeating because of the force of the message. As women, we often "split into two camps—the Marys and the Marthas . . . categorizing ourselves as either 'women who think' or 'women who serve,'" argues Custis-James. She, and I agree, does not dismiss the Marthas; practical women who "care passionately and actively for the needy hurting people around them" doing an "invaluable ministry." However, they also "suspect theology is over their heads and frankly are not all that interested." The "Marys, on the other hand, are most at home in the word of ideas. They relish an intellectual discussion," an unfortunate distinction between the two postures, leading women to think the two parts of life are "disconnected and incompatible instead of inseparably intertwined," a neglect for which women are paying a high price.[19]

In Luke 10:38–42, Christ commends as superior Mary's act of listening and giving attention to His presence even though it comes at the expense of household duty. He sees that Martha is distracted and disturbed by what she considers Mary's neglect of the work appropriate to her. Mary was not doing the traditionally "feminine" job; she was, in Sayers's words, "behaving just like any other disciple, male or female."[20] Christ analyzes the situation and says to Martha, "Martha, Martha, . . . you are worried and upset about many things, but only one thing is needed. Mary has chosen *what is better*, and it will not be taken away from her" (NIV, italics mine). Clearly, Christ encourages women to do what is better, which is to study at His feet.

In Mark 14:1–9, Christ again not only commends a woman's gift to Him, but He also refuses to tolerate criticism of her. In this account, the same Mary comes into a gathering of Jesus and His disciples and anoints Jesus' head with perfume. One could speculate that her action was controversial on several fronts. She came into a gathering of male leaders, Jesus and His disciples; she made what could be considered a scene by anointing Him; and she anointed Christ with an expensive perfume, an act considered wasteful by at least one if not more of the disciples (was that really the issue?).

Was Mary trying to cause trouble or get attention? Was she an early feminist? Or, was she so taken with Jesus, seen in other accounts, that she had to be near Him and give Him this gift she had planned so carefully? Was she suffused with an eternal longing? Some of the disciples, notably Judas Iscariot, as seen in the Matthew account, attack her harshly.

In what is a wonderfully comforting passage to any woman who has been put down or ignored, Christ immediately comes to Mary's defense and firmly rebukes her attackers, calling attention to their self-righteousness. He tells them to stop bothering her. But He goes further. He commends her gift as "beautiful" and makes her part of the approaching events of the Passion. And, in a wonderful ending, He asserts that her story will be told "throughout the world . . . in memory of her" (NIV). And, it is.

The names of other biblical women are probably familiar to you depending on your church and Bible background. You may even have a descriptive adjective in mind for each of them—the women who made wise decisions and others who are known for their destructive choices. As Alice Mathews, writing about biblical women, points out, "Decisions. We make them. Then they turn around and make us. Sometimes they break us." And it's not just the big decisions; it's the casual ones as well which, in her words, "sometimes turn out to be the most dramatic and life-changing of all."[21] The most obvious poor decision that comes to mind is Eve's, which is not, as Mathews says wryly, "just a decision about a piece of fruit. Or was it? Behind our little decisions often lurk big decisions. For Eve it was really a decision to doubt the goodness of God. It was a way of saying that God had misrepresented Himself, that He really did not have their best interests at heart."[22] Eve's theology was poor in the instant of her choice, and it introduced sin into the world.

Of course, many biblical women made excellent theological choices, like Hagar, Tamar, Rahab, Ruth, Naomi, Deborah, Hannah, Abigail, Esther, Huldah, Mary (the mother of Jesus), Mary of Bethany, the unnamed anointer in Luke 7, the prophetess Anna in Luke 2, the Syrophoenician woman in Matthew and Mark, Phoebe, Dorcas—the list goes on and on. And, yes, women's groups study some of them. We know that most of these women were submissive to God, a word that oversimplifies their commitment and the drama of their lives. In the case of the New Testament women, we know they were passionate about Jesus. But, just maybe when we picture them, we don't take them seriously; the passages including these women are often taught superficially, sometimes out of context. We may see them sitting quietly, subserviently, not engaged in theological conversations. We don't call them theologians any more than we think of ourselves as the same.

These women were edgy; they had dignity and character informed by knowledge. And when they suffered, that knowledge of God deepened.

Yet, if you look specifically at these biblical women, they were sustained by their knowledge of God or by listening to God when going through adversity. One-minute devotionals or coffee talks with Jesus wouldn't have done it. Abandoned and used, alone and pregnant, Hagar called upon God, and He not only provided food and water for her and her child, but He also enabled her to go back to Abram, which couldn't have been easy since Sarah, who had set up the sexual encounter between her and Abram, was still there. Rahab, a harlot, took great risks based on something she had heard, and her actions saved many Israelites. Ruth sought the theological instruction of her mother-in-law, Naomi, a woman who wrestled with God bitterly but was helped by her knowledge of His goodness. Attending to Naomi's instruction, Ruth listened, and her son is named in the lineage of Christ. Esther, believing the wisdom of her cousin Mordecai, heard the voice of God and submitted herself to a monster of a king because she believed in the God of Abraham, Isaac, and Jacob and knew the life and death of her people depended upon her faithful obedience.

In the New Testament, the pagan Syrophoenician woman approached Christ theologically to get healing for her daughter. Christ, impressed with her faith, not only healed her daughter but also used that faith as an example for others to follow. And the greatest example is Mary, the mother of Jesus, who at the age of fourteen if not younger, was able to submit herself to what must have been a terrifying calling and what would remain demanding beyond measure. She was selected deliberately because she had heard the word of the Lord and internalized it, giving her the discernment to obey God in the dark. Her knowledge of God steadied her. Her beautiful song in Luke 1, The Magnificat, is an indication of her theological understanding. That theology would ground her in the great hardship of having a son whose life would be unconventional and whom she would lose early, the Son who would be her Savior.

THEOLOGY INFORMS CHOICES

I can't repeat it enough. Theology informed these women's (women of all ages) choices and actions—they were not passive receptors. Their lives came under fire, and their deeply founded belief—real, truthful, and theological—led to choices that made a difference in how they are remembered in biblical history. These women were edgy; they had dignity and character informed by knowledge. And when they suffered, that knowledge of God deepened. In the words from the hymn "Take My Life and Let It Be" by Frances R. Havergal, "Take my intellect, and use/Every power as thou shalt choose."

These women fit the description given in the first chapter of *Jane Eyre*. They were "formidably self-possessed women with fully realized moral sensibilities"; they were "spirited," and perhaps their virtues would have been "off-putting" as principled decisions often are. They were theologians, and they are remembered with dignity. J. I. Packer has said it well in his widely read book, *Knowing God*: "The world becomes a strange, mad, painful place, and life in it a disappointing and unpleasant business, for those who do not know about God. Disregard the study of God, and you sentence yourself to stumble and blunder through life, blindfold, as it were, with no sense of direction and understanding of what surrounds you. This way you can waste your life, and lose your soul."[23]

Amy Carmichael, one of the great missionary stateswomen in history, certainly a theologian, was a pioneer in rescuing women from death, sexual abuse, and enforced prostitution. In her poem, "The Last Defile" she asks God to "make us Thy mountaineers," for "we would not linger on the lower slope." Perhaps to be "mountaineers" is to be students of God's Word, theologians, using the intellect, refusing the shallowness of "the lower slope."[24]

DISCUSSION QUESTIONS

1. What has been your view of theology and of the intellect? Spend some time thinking about that and writing down your answers.

2. Have you felt that you are part of the "invisible prejudice" described and if so, how?

3. What has been your experience with Bible study, both personal and in seminars and groups. What have been the weaknesses and strengths?

4. What can you do to become more theological?

SUGGESTED READING

- FICTION: *Christy* by Catherine Marshall.

- NONFICTION: *How to Read the Bible For All Its Worth* by Gordon Fee and Stuart Douglas. (This will teach you how to choose a Bible version and how to read correctly all the sections of the Bible and guide you to study resources.)

CHAPTER 5

DISTRACTED OR DIGNIFIED?
"Solid or Ghostly"

BY ROSALIE DE ROSSET

DISTRACTED: 1. Having the attention diverted.
2. Suffering conflicting emotions; distraught.

GENUINE: 1. Not spurious or counterfeit: authentic.
2. Free from hypocrisy or dishonesty: sincere.[1]

She was very showy, but she was not genuine: she had a fine person, many brilliant attainments; but her mind was poor, her heart barren by nature: nothing bloomed spontaneously on that soil; no unforced natural fruit delighted by its freshness. She was not good.[2]

JANE EYRE

She could not reconcile the anxieties of a spiritual life involving eternal consequences with a keen interest in gump and artificial protrusions of drapery.[3]

DOROTHEA

CHOOSING YOUR DESTINY

What kind of woman will you become? That is the central life question you must ask. The foundational premise established so far is that all your choices matter. If you choose the path of dignity, that means refusing to be a divided self, insisting on theological thinking, moral resolution, self-possession, and courage. It means maintaining a "detailed moral sensibility," a sense of voice, and a Christian understanding of your longing. Or you can become a product of your culture, like the description above, a woman with a "poor mind" and a "barren heart." To be young is to be standing at the crossroads of your life, whether you sense that or not. You don't have all the time in the world. Your choices make your destiny. What you will do with that life which is already well in progress, is colored by what you have chosen so far, perhaps carefully, perhaps casually or by default, the last postures the result of a deadly passivity. Probably, most of you are trying to figure it out.

In his allegorical work *The Great Divorce*, C. S. Lewis asks the reader: Will you be a solid person or a ghost? In this imaginative and theological set of connected stories, a newcomer to heaven, the narrator, is observing for the first time what is going on around him. He somehow finds himself in a grim and joyless city, the "grey town," either hell or purgatory, depending on how long one stays there. He eventually discovers a bus for the individuals who want to take a trip to another place, a place that turns out to be the foothills of heaven. The narrator gets on the bus and talks to the other passengers as they travel. When the bus reaches its destination, the passengers, including the narrator, are gradually revealed to be ghosts, insubstantial, wispy creatures. Although the place they have arrived is beautiful, every detail of the landscape, including the lakes and the grass, is solid compared to themselves. When they walk on the grass, they experience great pain; even a leaf is too heavy for them to lift.

Everything in the culture conspires to make us into shadows of something once alive.

Men and women the ghosts have known on earth meet them, shining figures who plead with them to repent so they can enter heaven. The shining figures offer to help the ghosts in the journey toward the mountains and the sunrise, promising they will grow more solid and hurt less. Sadly, most of the ghosts choose to go back to the grey town for any number of reasons, most of them excuses and evasions. Self-deception has turned them into shadows; they will not give up their familiar sins and defenses to experience heavenly reality and joy.

Each chapter of the allegory presents a different ghost with a new but familiar kind of defense he or she must surrender in order to become a real person. The most pitiful, the narrator tells us, is a female ghost who

> . . . appeared to be contorting her all but invisible face and writhing her smokelike body in a quite meaningless fashion. At last I came to the conclusion—incredible as it seemed—that she supposed herself still capable of attracting them and was trying to do so. She was a thing that had become incapable of conceiving conversation save as a means to that end. If a corpse already liquid with decay had arisen from the coffin, smeared its gums with lipstick, and attempted a flirtation, the result could not have been more appalling. In the end she muttered, "Stupid creatures," and turned back to the bus.[4]

This rather horrible picture is of a woman who, seduced by her culture and its twisted values, has lived an overstimulated, unreflective life, found her values in what everyone around her was doing, and who has remained obsessed with appearance. In the end, like the woman described in the quote which starts this chapter, "she [is] not good; she [is] not original . . . truth and tenderness are not in her." She is a distracted woman, an artificial woman, finally, not a woman at all. She is a ghost.

One can see them everywhere: women who are ghosts, young and old, who while living shrilly are still examples of voicelessness, of the divided soul, of longing gone wrong. Everything in the culture conspires to make us into ghosts ("a light trace or bit"),[5] into shadows of something once alive. And, very sadly, too often we aren't even stopping to ask questions about what might be thinning out our humanity, at the core of which is what we believe. Faith lite is not faith at all. I can't say it with enough emphasis: you can't afford to be casual about any part of your life. The misplacement of longing, the mistaking of the temporal for the eternal will always turn you into a ghost.

Just make a list sometime of the actresses who, while still beautiful, disappear from the scene before they turn forty.

What the female ghost is obsessed with is being attractive and, perhaps, that awful word we use, with being "sexy" or its more recent version "hot." What no doubt started as a natural desire to be appealing became a priority then an obsession, finally growing monstrous and turning her into a ludicrous shadow of a person. Every one of us has seen older women wearing too much makeup, dressing too young, so consumed with holding back time that they have lost sight of dignity. They are ghosts. However, one can also see the beginnings of the ghostliness in young women, even beautiful, young women in their concentration on physical image no matter what it costs in time or money, completely self-preoccupied, no matter how much it steals from other more significant and lasting facets of personal development.

PRIORITIZING BEAUTY: THE DARK CONSEQUENCES
The effect of prioritizing beauty as a value has had dark effects ranging from simmering personal dissatisfaction to the muted

depression many girls and women live with. I suspect almost every woman, young or old, knows the despair that comes over her after she has looked at a woman's magazine, perhaps in passing in a drugstore, while waiting for an appointment at a doctor's office, or at a hair salon. The images tell women that if they make enough effort and self-sacrifice, they can be the culture's ideal which includes unnatural thinness, glowing skin, wide eyes, and big hair, all illustrated with an airbrushed, digitally rendered model.

Of course, such a transformation is impossible for most people and certainly cannot last. Just make a list sometime of the actresses who, while still beautiful, disappear from the scene before they turn forty. In my lifetime there have been scores. Seduced, however, women find themselves a lot poorer, as the misuse of money is inevitable if one is obsessed with physical appearance. How many women have a drawer full of products that testify to this seduction, to the surrender to a profound lie? Look for a minute at your own stash. What does it tell you? I'm reminded of the words from the 1968 musical *Funny Girl*: "If a girl isn't pretty/She should get a job,/ Go get a job—/get any job/get a weekly pay/'Cause if a girl isn't pretty/Like a Miss Atlantic City/She's a real Miss Nobody U.S.A."

Whether we have thought very long about this or not, I think most of us recognize the tension between what we see presented to us as the cultural ideal and what is in our souls if we have made a commitment to a Christian way of living. If there is no discord, that is a deeper problem. In an editorial for a Christian college newspaper, one young student wrote about the conflict in her spirit: "I stop at a Borders . . . colorful publications lure me into thinking that if I read the magazine's contents, I'll be able to: reduce my stress level in half, lose ten pounds of pure fat . . . sculpt my back sexy, get any man I want and drive him crazy in bed, de-jiggle sagging facial muscles, and make millions. But another cover picture I had seen that day lingers in my mind. There are few Albanian refugee women who haven't been brutally raped. . . . What, if by some bizarre irony, the Albanian women with their oily hair and sagging facial muscles made it on the cover of *Self.* It would upset subscribers, take them out of a frivolous fantasy."[6]

I remember reading Cinderella and worrying about my foot size. I knew the glass slipper would not fit me.

Here, well-described, is the reality every woman sees looking at her from every corner. I read once in a professional beauty handbook that few to none of these products do what they claim, no matter what the price. In fact, said this writer, when it comes to moisturizers, any woman would do just as well to use lard on her face, a product that costs pennies a night. Websites and magazines devoted to objective reporting on these products confirm that statement. As a young woman with limited resources, I once used Crisco on my face for a few weeks. It worked just fine, though the aesthetics left a great deal to be desired.

More serious is the effect on girls and women of the standard for body size projected by fashion advertising. A researcher at Brigham and Women's Hospital in Boston discovered that "the more frequently girls read magazines, the more likely they were to diet and to feel that magazines influence their ideal body shape." Almost one-half of them talked about wanting to lose weight because of a magazine picture, and only 29 percent of these girls were actually overweight. Furthermore, a growing percentage of very young girls, even preteens, are actively trying to lose weight.[7] It is no wonder that some professionals have noted a correlation between depression and the habit of looking at too many of those magazines. Jean Kilbourne calls this lie "deadly persuasion" in her frightening book on the power of advertising over girls' and women's lives. This "tendency," she writes, "to view one's body from the outside in—regarding physical attractiveness, sex appeal, measurements, and weight as more central to one's physical identity than health, strength, energy level, coordination, or fitness—has many harmful effects, including diminished mental performance, increased feelings of shame and anxiety, depression, sexual dysfunction, and the development of eating disorders."[8]

Susan Shapiro Barash appears to agree with Kilbourne when she lists the magazine headlines from such sources as *Harper's Bazaar*, *Marie Claire*, and *InStyle*, not to mention *Seventeen*. She writes, "The message is clear: women are judged relentlessly, not only by how we look but by how we measure up to an impossibly rigid set of standards." Then she goes on to discuss the terrible competition that such a value must give birth to. In her interviews with many, many girls and women, she reports that 80 percent felt competitive with other women over physical appearance. And even in the group of women who, as she puts it, "didn't define themselves by their appearance," the subject of looks was a painful area, causing self-loathing.[9] Starting even with certain fairy tales, women are judged relentlessly for their appearance. I once read an essay in which the writer deconstructs the Cinderella story, arguing that she makes it because she is drop-dead gorgeous and, very important to the story, she has small feet. I remember reading Cinderella and worrying about my foot size. I knew the glass slipper would not fit me.[10]

Perhaps the plastic surgery, resculpting, skin bleaching, and non-surgical procedures of every kind common even among very young women today are a modern version of the terrible practice of foot-binding in China. My grandparents, who were in ministry for fifty years and four of whose six children went to foreign missions, often had missionaries in their home. As a result, my grandmother had a china closet full of artifacts from all over the world. When I cleaned out that closet as the house was being sold, I found a tiny shoe, no more than six inches long, a shoe from China used on a foot that had been bound.

Lisa See has written an unforgettable novel called *Snow Flower and the Secret Fan* about, among other things, the terrible effects of that practice on Chinese women. A ritual enforced upon young adolescents by their mothers and grandmothers, the girls' toes were bent back and bound more tightly every few days until the appropriate foot size was achieved, and the girls could walk on what was almost a stump. This meant that bones broke, bleeding occurred, and violent pain ensued. One in ten of these girls died from the procedure. And when the revolution came, many of the women could not run away. All to make the future husband "a happy man," for a small foot had sexual power in that culture.[11] While contemporary physical mutilations may not be so severe and are not mandated, the spirits of women everywhere are showing the consequences of chosen mutilations, external and internal, ones which also keep them frozen in place, unable to run. It would probably be a good thing for each of us to ask ourselves, how do we indulge in a kind of mutilation?

PRIORITIZING BEAUTY IN THE CHRISTIAN WORLD

I remind my readers of these familiar realities because the obsession doesn't affect just those who don't know Christ; the emphasis on appearance crosses all boundaries. In fact, it seems possible at times to ask, "Is Christianity Only Meant for Pretty Women?", a question that at first seems outrageous. We look at those words again. Surely, we want to think, Christian women will be valued, at least in theory, for their sweetness, submissiveness, ministry-involvement, and purity, an incomplete list at best but less "secular." Then, we think again and realize we have felt that question somewhere inside of ourselves more than we'd like to admit. This question actually forms the title of an article written a couple of decades ago for the *Wittenberg Door*, a Christian satire magazine. Dave Peterson and a group of his colleagues looked closely at the image of Christian women on the covers of five Christian women's magazines and almost two hundred Christian books, including romance/historical novels, Bible stories, youth fiction, and youth nonfiction. Of the 165 magazine pictures they observed, 96 of the women in them were either knockouts or above-average looking, and 48 were average-looking. One has to wonder about the meaning of average in this setting. Only two older women, older presumably being over forty, were featured.[12]

"I discovered a grand total of two older women, one overweight female, one female wearing glasses, and one female with braces. Zits did not exist in this world."

Worse yet for the average woman was the presentation of women on Christian book covers because these illustrations are more easily idealized than photographs. One hundred six of those images, says Peterson, "would easily be classed as knockouts by any male with normal-functioning eyes." To get specific, sixty-seven of the pictures were of above-average looking women, and only fifteen of them came close to being average-looking. He adds, "I discovered a grand total of two older women, one overweight female, one female wearing glasses, and one female with braces. Zits did not exist in this world."[13]

While this unofficial study is not recent, it seems unarguable that the results would be more discouraging if the same research were conducted today because the stakes continue to get higher. Current representations are even more ideal than they were, the women visualized younger, sometimes dangerously young, and more glamorous. Glaringly obvious is that Christian culture as represented through its media outlets and public personalities (including speakers and musicians), has chosen to present some of the same values as secular culture with just a little alteration. For sure, youth and looks matter, at least by implication. And they *seem* at times to matter more than what is in the heart and the soul. That's when one begins to see that the question, "Is Christianity Only Meant for Pretty Women?" is not so far-fetched.

To summarize his findings, Peterson quotes Quentin Schultze, communications and social media specialist: "While our culture's ideal woman is 'a cross between a prostitute and a good-looking homemaker,' the Christian ideal woman is 'domestic' with just 'a mild edge of sensuality.'"[14] Today, with lowered standards of modesty in almost every circle, another important discussion, perhaps those two categories are closer than originally analyzed.

What such skewed practices demonstrate is that Christian culture is not helping women connect their bodies and spirit, a bridge that is theologically crucial to living an authentic Christian life. In an insightful novel called *Feeling for Bones*, author Bethany Pierce tells the poignant story of Olivia, a teenager who is working through her family dysfunction as it has affected her physical and spiritual life. Suffering with an eating disorder, she is haunted by her image as she sees it in mirrors and in reflecting surfaces of all kinds. As an antidote, she covers her bedroom walls with slick clippings from glamour magazines. At one point she turns to *Paradise Lost* and reads the lines, "The mind is its own place, and in itself/ Can make a heaven of hell, a hell of heaven." Then she thinks to herself, "My personal hell existed within the confines of my skull. I'd gone beyond thinking my body was the trouble. The real culprit, I knew, was the mind. But I'd never considered my fear a spiritual matter. I didn't understand that the body and the spirit are connected, that the abuse and suffering of one affects the other, wind to the belly of the kite. They move together."

She continues:

I'd spent every ounce of my mental power counting the calories in my food. . . . I'd never given my imagination leave to flirt with the idea of God. Didn't the Bible speak of angels doing battle? Of Christ resplendent in glory? Of the church as a living body? These ideas had been lost to me beneath the felt figurines of Sunday school lectures. If God were the God Christians claimed Him to be, surely He would shoot adrenaline down the very fibers of my soul. I went to bed thinking of angels conferencing, of spirits scheming, of the Garden dripping with sensual delight.[15]

Then, Olivia thinks wistfully, oh if there were just such a living kingdom, made of real visions. Of course, there is, but how little we hear about it in a way that compels us. When one reads passages in the Bible that include significant women, only a few are said to be beautiful, and that beauty is never the most important thing about them. Their dress is mentioned only in general terms or in connection with modesty. The women who are most commended did significant things, obeying God at great personal risk and expense; they "treasured things in their heart" like Mary, the mother of Jesus. Or they sat at the feet of Christ engaging Him in what I feel sure was an active conversation. I think we imagine Mary, the mother of Jesus and Mary of Bethany as beautiful. How do you picture them and other biblical women? After years of studying and reading the Bible, I still see them in silhouette, looking demure and "godly," their long hair shining down their backs covering a part of their faces.

One wonders, then, if there had been magazines and novels in Bible times, how many of the women would have been attractive enough to be featured on the cover.

The reality is that we have no idea what these women looked like. Even Esther is more notable for her intelligent and godly cooperation with her cousin Mordecai and her earnest prayer to God than for her beauty. And as described earlier, the beautiful Abigail was wise in her handling of a complex situation, the emphasis of that biblical account. These women had noble characters, bearing, conduct, and speech, all of which adds up to dignity. And clearly, they had a vision of God that infused them with wonder. One wonders, then, if there had been magazines and novels in Bible times, how many of the women would have been attractive enough to be featured on the cover.

THE TEMPTATION OF IMAGE

The temptation to feel worth through external appearance is one of the temptations women face, temptations that come not usually out of pride, but out of not feeling good about themselves. A kind of greed nags at women's lives, writes Mary Ellen Ashcroft, a "pathetic" greed that starts young. She writes, "Our inner self becomes like the mythical dragon that demands more and more maidens to fill it. . . . The monster will not be satisfied."[16] As one of my colleagues put it, "Finding our identity in gendered distractions precludes finding our identity in Christ."[17] The inevitable ending of a life lived so is ghostliness.

Even more dangerous are the omnipresent sexual messages that lurk behind much advertising, carving subtle grooves into girls' and women's consciousness. More and more, the messages are not subtle. In the last twenty-five years, an explosion of franchises has arisen devoted to body scents, makeups, and lingerie. Large malls and major city streets have any number of these stores. Particularly visible and toxic is Victoria's Secret, whose windows present what is really soft pornography and sometimes the disturbing combination of religious symbols and sex as in the display of Victoria's angels. If we buy an item at this store, the catalogue arrives shortly thereafter, picturing scores of seductive models standing coyly in provocative poses or draped on couches in positions one wonders how they sustain without spraining something.

But, we are seduced, pushing down spiritual conviction to accommodate what everyone is doing. We walk by, looking into the window at the sumptuous, anorexically thin yet well-endowed model only to glance down hesitantly at ourselves, feeling a kind of despair. Perhaps, though, something in there will make me look more beautiful, we tell ourselves. Oddly enough, only a handful of times have I heard anyone talk publicly about whether or not a Christian woman should shop at Victoria's Secret though I have had the conversation with a number of women in private. Most Christian women I talk to never did or don't think about it anymore. Or I've heard them argue that the lingerie in the store fits well. Okay, but it's not as though there's a lack of places to find intimate wear. Every major department store carries a substantial, varied, and attractive collection without such blatant soft-porn messages or invitations to compare ourselves to an impossible standard. Interestingly, the women I know who have started to think about the subject are often married and have discovered that their husbands have a pornography problem. Suddenly, this kind of catalogue doesn't seem so neutral. Combine that with the V.S. ads on television and the annual modeling show, and one can see the philosophical motivation.

About the time I stopped being able to go into the store even to buy the lotions I had used for a while, I saw the first objection to Victoria's Secret. It was not so much about the moral compromise involved but about the objectification of women, the woman-as-whore image that Victoria's Secret encourages, something that has nothing to do with how God calls men to view women or women to view themselves.

While speaking at a college in California, I picked up a copy of the student newspaper and was caught by a title, "Protesting

Victoria." In it, a young woman columnist opens the editorial with these words: "The most incensing piece of mail I receive, the most damaging to women, is a catalogue supposedly catering to women." She goes on to analyze the images the catalogue presents, the deceptively "innocent airhead look," the "sexpot vixen pose," the "come-n-get-me" look, and the get-up, including black stiletto heels that suggests bondage. "It seems more targeted toward a hormonally hyperactive male audience," she suggests, "as evinced by the countless number of men who borrow copies from their girlfriends" (this last reality a sad commentary on how much women have lost their way). "It is time," the writer concludes, "we women stopped submitting to this idea. Who wants the clinging, dependent, spineless airhead held up as the feminine ideal." Then she calls for women on campus to cancel their subscriptions with a letter that tells why.[18]

On another occasion I heard a young, very attractive talk show host urge mothers to watch where their young daughters were shopping and what they were shopping for—her example was Victoria's Secret. Whatever you decide about shopping there or anywhere else, ask yourself hard questions about why you go there and what you want, what the atmosphere makes you think about and feel, and whether or not you can defend your choice of place or product theologically and philosophically. For, as Ashcroft concludes, "Satan must be delighted to have so much money, emotional energy and time spent pursuing the meaningless mirage of the ideal woman's body."[19]

CONFUSING MESSAGES

Life in America is particularly hard on women. Everything seems to be about the importance of having a relationship, about physical beauty, and about success. Sometimes Christian parents put undue physical expectations on their daughters. And, sadly, as noted, Christian magazines don't do a whole lot better than mainstream magazines when it comes to a realistic portrayal of girls and women. And what is really confusing is that the same Christian magazine littered with glamorous images will likely present articles emphasizing character and other biblical virtues. This kind of journalistic schizophrenia abets the divided self. But the underlying supposition is that if a less-than-conventionally attractive woman were to appear on the cover of a magazine, book, or in an article illustration, unless she were famous, somehow there would be no, what they call in real estate, "curb appeal."

British journalist Malcolm Muggeridge may have been right when he made the judgment that Christians have "adjusted to current depravity."

We haven't scrutinized these ironies enough, corporately or individually. Not only must the church be ruthless in examining the values it has adopted about the ideal woman from the wider culture, but each one of us must also do an inventory of our lives, noting our obsessions and the things we do to feed them. As I watch young women torn by the conflict between earthly and eternal values, as I watch the confusion in their lives, I long for the leaders, men and women, of our Christian media outlets, publishing houses, national and local conferences, and institutions to speak prophetically. I long for them to think about what they present not only to all women, but particularly to young Christian women who are in formation, whose choices about every facet of their lives will make a big difference to their future. Struggling with how to think about themselves, to discern what is important, beset powerfully by the omnipresence of shallow cultural images, they may too often find the same emphasis in all things Christian including their churches and their influences. British journalist Malcolm Muggeridge may have been right when he made the judgment that Christians have "adjusted to current depravity."[20] Which is why you have to have your theology straight, why you have to be wary, why you must reason as well as feel.

SLOTH AND THE PURSUIT OF THE TRIVIAL

The problem is that those things that are really important in the one life given us to live can be suffocated by the pursuit of the trivial and corrupt. Its urgency may dominate our thinking, a twisted, self-focused ideology that is incompatible with true creativity and spiritual depth, finally a kind of "sloth," the fourth on the list of the seven deadly sins in Christendom. The word really means a desire for ease at the expense of doing the will of God in every area of life, large or small. "Originally," Ashcroft tells us, "sloth meant 'spiritual lethargy.' Sloth implied that a person was lazy about Christian growth." She cites Jesus' teaching that we must not "work for the food that perishes, but for the food that endures for eternal life, which the Son of Man will give to you" (John 6:27). But, as she so rightly observes, "Tempted by sloth, we are tempted to forget that our time and talents are gifts from God to be used for him. We begin to think that time is ours to kill or fill at our own discretion" even though as Paul tells us, "You are not your own, for you were bought with a price" (1 Corinthians 6:19–20).[21]

The truth is that anything worthwhile we do in life demands effort. I often use the picture of a tightrope walker at a circus to illustrate the readiness with which our lives are to be lived. At the top of the tent, without a trampoline under them, tightrope walkers launch out across the wire for the other side, their arms held out for balance, a balance that requires utter mental concentration and the tautness of every muscle in their bodies. Their lives depend on that kind of focus and discipline. Without it, they fall to serious injury or death. Our spiritual lives in Christ also depend on our focus, on the tautness of our spiritual muscles. No area of our lives is neutral territory or can allow laziness.

In the novella *The Awakening* by Kate Chopin, the lead character, Edna Pontellier, having lived her life in a romantic illusion, a sloth which destroys her, says, "The years that are gone seem like dreams—if one might go on sleeping and dreaming—but to wake up and find—oh! Well! Perhaps it is better to wake up after all, even to suffer, rather than to remain a dupe to illusions all one's life."[22] I go back again to the presenting question, "What kind of woman will you become?" Will you resist the seduction of prioritizing beauty and sexiness, your spiritual and mental muscles taut, or will you fill and kill time relentlessly pursuing what cannot last, gaining the illusory approval that has a short shelf life, what will in time certainly leave you ghostly and empty. It is no accident that the expression is "kill time"; such obsessions do indeed infuse time and life with death.

A WORD ON SELF-COMMAND

Of course, beneath most of our desires is a need for significance, to be normal, and to be loved. For most women who become fixated on appearance, there is also the component of having influence over a man or men and, finally, the desire to be with a man, something which women often think will help them be taken seriously (too often a reality) as well as fill the deepest longings of their hearts. While understandable, this desire can be terribly distorted if one allows it to define one's personhood.

That dangerous distortion is what Jane Austen wants to illustrate in *Sense and Sensibility*. She wants women to understand the beauty of reserve, containment, or what she calls "self-command." The story and films based on the novel teach women the difference between distracted/undignified and undistracted/dignified living by contrasting sharply the two main female characters. Marianne wears her intense, often immature feelings on her sleeve, throwing herself spontaneously, almost unthinkingly into relationships with men. At first colorful and attractive, her carelessness about herself and others betrays her selfishness, and she becomes annoying. She is "everything but prudent," we're told. Having believed the lie that being absorbed into a man is the goal, the way to happiness, Marianne becomes sick and isolated until she learns some hard lessons.[23]

In contrast, Elinor is full of prudence, caution, reserved understanding, good judgment, and she possesses "an excellent heart." As one critic puts it, Elinor knows how to "govern" her feelings; her discretion never lets her be presumptuous about a man's feelings for her which always stands her in good stead. She would never pick up the phone too soon, ask him to "define the relationship," or make herself too visible. Always showing insight, she guards her heart and maintains her self-respect. She has good sense. Unlike Marianne, she is an independent, undistracted thinker.[24]

Though her story ends well, Marianne is in a position to make a lot of serious mistakes. She has subscribed to some of the myths or errors in judgment that strip women of their dignity and mystique. Christian speaker and author Mary Whelchel lists a number of ways in which I have seen women show their desperation and in doing so seriously open themselves up to disrespect and poor dating patterns. Some of these are seeing marriage as the only normal way to live, "misinterpreting the attentions of the opposite sex, putting up with too much in a relationship or hang[ing] on too long, misreading danger signals,[25] getting physically involved too soon and going too far, imagining that the only requirement for a date or mate is that he or she is a Christian."[26] I would add to that the dangers of moving too fast and of isolating yourself within the relationship. All of these demonstrate belief in the lie that anything is better than being alone.

Elinor will not succumb to desperation, the queen of all distractions, a disregard for self as made whole in God's image. Desperation can only end desperately in the fate of the ghostly woman in the passage cited early who is "still writhing her smokelike body in a quite meaningless fashion," hoping for a flirtation and unable to have a conversation except to get the affirmation she craves.

DISCUSSION QUESTIONS

1. In what ways have you prioritized beauty and body image, and what has it led you to do that might be a problem? Has it led you to sloth?

2. What is your philosophy of shopping, and does it have a biblical component? Keep a journal of what you spend and the motivation behind it.

3. Are you more like Marianne or Elinor? Can you see the difference in dignity?

4. How have you envisioned the biblical women you have heard or read about? Write a paragraph describing that, then turn to the biblical passage to see what this woman is remembered for.

SUGGESTED READING

- FICTION: *Feeling for Bones* by Bethany Pierce.

- NONFICTION: *Deadly Persuasion: Why Women and Girls Must Fight the Addictive Power of Advertising.* Now called *Can't Buy My Love* by Jean Kilbourne.

CHAPTER 6

MINDFUL OR MINDLESS
A Theology of Play

BY ROSALIE DE ROSSET

CLASSIC: 1. Of the highest rank or class. 2. Serving as an outstanding representative of its kind, model. 3. Having lasting significance or recognized worth.[1]

LEISURE: 1. Freedom from time-consuming duties, responsibilities, or activities.[2]

She was not original; she used to repeat sounding phrases from books: she never offered, nor had, an opinion of her own. She advocated a high tone of sentiment; but she did not know the sensations of sympathy and pity; tenderness and truth were not in her.[3]

JANE EYRE

Whatever is true, whatever is noble, whatever is right, whatever is pure, whatever is lovely, whatever is admirable—if anything is excellent or praiseworthy—think about such things.

PHILIPPIANS 4:8 (NIV)

When I was in high school in the sixties, I went around with a little blue transistor radio glued to my head, the iPod of its day. I still have it. The radio had been my sister's, and I'm afraid to say I appropriated it. I had discovered pop music, and it had its grip on me. As I moved from crush to crush, heat to heat, including my history teacher, my band director, and a boy called Billy, I sang the songs that brought them to mind. I knew all the words—"Johnny Angel, how I love him, how I tingle when he passes by, every time he says 'Hello' my heart begins to fly." No linguistic brilliance there. You have probably never heard the song. No loss, I might add.

In 1964, the Beatles had arrived, and by then my longing was for a boy named Frank, and with the Beatles, "I wanted to hold his hand." A little later, when I sat in study hall, in Frank's line of vision, and he wouldn't even look my way, I went home and agonized to the tune of Simon and Garfunkel's "I am a rock, I am an island, and a rock feels no pain, and an island never cries."

At sixteen I discovered *Gone With the Wind*, and by the time I went to college, I had read it eight times, a reality which probably meant I needed a little counseling. I was even prepared to write the sequel. I could quote paragraphs from it. I wish I had put that energy into memorizing Scripture and Shakespeare. I thought about the way Rhett looked at Scarlett as though he knew her, knew her in a way no one else could or would. He knew her cruelty, her insecurity, her vanity, her girlhood, and her womanhood. Still, he loved her. It was *eros* and *storge* together, the longings of body and soul, family and affection conjoined. I suppose I was looking for a Christian Rhett. For sure, I was a sucker for "the look." Of course, what this was all about was longing. As has been said, such longing is about our souls, not our present reality; the circumstances of life, be it a beautiful sunrise, lovely music, or the excitement of a new relationship are but portals to heaven for the Christian, portals we must not become lodged in or we will miss the point.

In my home church there were historians, keepers of the gate, guardians of my soul.

It was that time of life—teenagehood with much heady ecstasy, writing free verse in my journal, feeling sad at sunsets and in love (or in something) just about all the time. All very normal, kind of wonderful, but incomplete, something that had to mature and change. In youth group we sang some dumb songs: "Do Lord, oh do Lord, oh do remember me." "Kumbaya my Lord, Kumbaya." We sat around the campfire part of the time and cast our twigs into the fire and warbled, "It only takes a spark to get a fire going." Not exactly poetic wonders. No one sings them now. Don't laugh—wait till you see what you think of your songs in twenty years. But the little blue radio was not always on, and in my home church there were historians, keepers of the gate, guardians of my soul—those who understood that people my age should not run the format of a church or be the measure of what is important. These were the people who understood that when adolescent heat and trendiness pass, we must retain in our memories something bigger and better, something not adolescent to have in our keeping as treasures for when we grew up. They made sure our inheritance was not swallowed up by what seemed important in the sixties or at sixteen. These guardians of our souls knew that popular trends and teenage moods come and go, and that they must give us a solid memory and understanding of what was better, more mature, classic.

GUARDIANS OF THE SOUL

The church and my parents were the keepers of my mind, and finally of my soul. The job had been entrusted to them by God, and they took it seriously, making sure we not only knew the great hymns but also what they meant, or in my parents' case, making sure I knew the great novels and that my mind did not turn into mush or sentimental nonsense. They understood that our failure to remember leads to a dangerous kind of intellectual and spiritual amnesia. They wanted their children's lives to be dignified. The eloquent commentator Charles Krauthammer puts it well when he says one of the marks of this technological era is that "everyone finds themselves living in an ever-moving pastless present in which the first casualty is memory." He ends the article by saying, "If the Ten Commandments were given today, they would be flashed on the great Diamond Vision Screen at Yankee Stadium and by sunup not a soul would remember them."[4]

Today many of you are not so lucky as I was. There are fewer and fewer historians, guardians of the soul in our churches, homes, and Christian institutions. Sometimes I think adults aren't doing their duty in warning or protecting young adults lovingly. They seem to be intimidated. More and more the "contemporary" dominates the scene—the latest book, the latest music, the latest CCM group— with little regard for history as it manifests itself in the great classics, the great hymns, and in great art. One of our great idolatries, yours and mine, comes from our loss of memory, of respect for the past; we become locked in the present moment, no longer able to judge and discern the good from the mediocre. We forget in the entertainment of the moment to bring with us the best of what God's gifted men and women have given us, and to maintain a standard for what we will do now and in the future. Sadder still, sometimes we may not even be interested.

You must look at the contents of your life through a theological lens, including what you do with your leisure.

Today, tradition has come to have negative connotations—it conjures up out-of-date services, heavy reading, old-fashioned clothes, the older service on a Sunday morning. But what is tradition really? Marva Dawn, author of the very important book *Reaching Out Without Dumbing Down*, defines it well: "Tradition is the process," she writes, "by which one generation passes on its accumulated wisdom, stories, and values to another."[5] Think about that—"the process by which one generation passes on its accumulated wisdom, stories, and values to another." One of my questions to you today is what have you accumulated from the past—what are you in the process of accumulating that will be passed on, if not deliberately, then accidentally? Is this accumulation the best of what has been and the best of what is currently being written, sung, and created? Is it wise? And if not, what will be the next generation's inheritance, your children's legacy?

How much thought have you put into what you do for fun?

What my parents understood was that "everything is theological,"[6] a sentence I used to see on the office door of a colleague and whose truth has stayed with me. Everything must be filtered through your knowledge of who God is, what He teaches is best for those who know Him—everything you do, not just your Bible study, devotional life, attention to church duties, or moral behavior. Everything includes church and home, relationships of all kinds, work and play. Yes, play. You must look at the contents of your life through a theological lens, including what you do with your leisure. Do you even have a philosophy of leisure? Or are you wondering what on earth I'm talking about? You will not be alone in wondering. And maybe, the word *leisure* itself needs to be explained.

A PHILOSOPHY OF LEISURE

What comes to your mind when you think of leisure? How do you define it? Stop a minute and write down the answer to that question. The dictionary's definition of the word *leisure* is "freedom from time-consuming duties, responsibilities, or activities."[7] "Downtime" is what I hear many people calling it. Having a philosophy of leisure, of downtime means that, as a Christian, you have thought theologically and biblically about what you do with the time you call your own, with what you choose as entertainment, what you do when you relax. If you don't, what you consider leisure may very well just be idleness. Okay, maybe some of you don't think you have much leisure. But, really, we are a leisured society whether we realize it or not—our busyness is often chosen, not necessary to our survival as it once was.

Sadly, while a fairly extensive written and spoken discussion exists to guide you in matters of ministry, calling, and work, almost nothing is written about a philosophy, let alone a theology of leisure. The discussion should actually start much earlier in your lives than it does; every youth group and Sunday school class would be enriched by such a conversation. Certainly, preachers, teachers, conference and seminar speakers seldom talk about it. Though I have given such a talk, I have seldom if ever heard a lecture on the subject. Thankfully, some good books on the topic have been written.

How much time do you spend *not* connected technologically, *not* watching something—in solitude or silence?

Of course, many of us know the things we're not supposed to do, but aside from the obvious (and are they really so obvious anymore?) problematic entertainments and activities that a given family or Christian community thinks are wrong, how much thought have you put into what you do for fun? Even the category of what is wrong differs widely and sadly is becoming an increasingly irrelevant discussion, an overreaction to the fear of legalism. Having gone to church faithfully, participated in Bible studies, volunteered at the local soup kitchen, mentored someone younger, and even gone on a summer mission trip, you feel free to do your thing. And perhaps that part of your life happens almost randomly, a product of feeling not thinking.

"Even just standing on the corner of a street waiting for the light to change, I felt the strongest urge to text."

You can't afford to be casual about any part of your life, or you will be in the words of one writer, a "mindless nibbler." As I look at today's Christian world, so many questions go unasked. Do you go along with your particular group or follow the trends of the culture, including today's inordinate technological distraction? How much of your leisure is taken up with using the Internet, texting friends, updating Facebook status reports, shopping, or watching movies? Though broadly popular, these things are not benign or neutral. Many of these activities aren't only subtly unrelational (they depend on screen distance; managed, self-focused image; and avoiding the person-to-person contact that includes risk), but they also discourage reflection as they are unarguably time consuming and busy. Have you thought about what your distractions keep you from, what you would do if they weren't available, or how necessary they have become to your life? What indiscretions and/or embarrassments have they led you to, either written (careless emails or texts you can't take back), verbal (talking on a cell phone where someone could overhear something private), or relational (too much contact too soon)? Is any portion of your time spent in good conversation sitting across the table from a person? How much time do you spend *not* connected technologically, *not* watching something—in solitude or silence? What role do dignity and character play in your choice of activities?

FASTING FROM MEDIA

For several years, I have asked an English class to do a media fast over five consecutive days. The students cannot use their cell phones (even to call/text family, unless they are married), listen to music, use the Internet except for school assignments, go on Facebook, or watch television and movies. At the same time, they must keep a journal, recording what they discover about themselves in the process. With the exception of a few students, the findings are telling and remarkably similar. Most students admit they find themselves nervous and "bored" at first, even irritated or angry. Many of them simply didn't know what to do with "downtime," even during short waiting times. One student said, "Even just standing on the corner of a street waiting for the light to change, I felt the strongest urge to text . . . like I had this dependency on wanting to feel . . . connected . . . or comfort in knowing that someone wants to talk to me, ask my opinion, see where I am." More than one student wrote about the spiritual implications of this dependency. "The tragedy for me was realizing how much I feel like I need it. Being updated on what everyone is doing in my social sphere has become somewhat of an idol. I could boldly say Facebook at times is my source of peace. I only feel it when I know everything is okay with my friends because Facebook told me."[8]

A large number of students experienced relief at not having to be in touch with so many people ("It feels liberating to be disconnected with the rest of the world"), even their parents, all the time. After about the third day, some of them talked about how much more time they had to study and read, how much more effort it took to actually see someone, how much better a face-to-face conversation was, how much time they realized they wasted in trivial activity ("I have wasted hours upon hours of my life on Facebook, email, and music") and how deep the consequences were in their lives because of the better things these nervous and compulsive habits replaced. One student summed up the issues well: "It was as if I had ceased treatment of a very-low-dosed drug that made me somewhat dull, hazy, and numb. The days seemed brighter, more real, and more important. I was drowning in Media."

While most of these students go back to their familiar, even addictive patterns, a few actually give up some facet of what they have been doing. Apparent is that technology, which has greatly enhanced many processes and institutions but weakened others, is controlling us; we are without a philosophical and theological basis for thinking about it.[9] It has never occurred to most people that what one does with technology may also be a spiritual discipline.

While every generation has had its distractions, distraction is the great distinctive of the time in which we are living. Richard Winter, in a book called *Still Bored in a Culture of Entertainment*, talks about the "deadness of soul" that haunts this generation, "a world where so much is happening that it is hard to keep up and make sense of it all" . . . where "stimulation comes at us from every side," until "we cannot respond with much depth to anything" because we are "bombarded with so much that is exciting and demands our attention, we tend to become unable to discriminate and choose from among the many options." We are, in effect, overstimulated by the possibilities of technology, entertainment, and advertising.[10]

UNDERSTANDING LEISURE

So, contrary to what a lot of people think, what we do with our leisure can have more effect on us than what we do purposefully. In fact, writes Josef Pieper, the author of an older but still pertinent classic treatment of the subject, "Leisure [is] a condition of the soul." Why? Because it is "a form of stillness that is the necessary preparation for accepting reality; only the person who is still can hear, and whoever is not still, cannot hear."[11] The assumption here is that what encourages stillness and true reflection becomes true pleasure. A great deal that we do is not leisured but a kind of working at pleasure that can be nervous idleness. Yet, what we do purely for pleasure may have the greatest and least suspect influence on us. What we do with the least effort can be insidious. As obedient Christians, we protect ourselves against obvious evils. Our guard is up if only a little; if we haven't thought about a matter, we aren't defended.

In a book on fasting, John Piper talks about this plainly when he says, "The greatest enemy of hunger for God is not poison but apple pie. It is not the banquet of the wicked that dulls our appetite for heaven, but *endless* [emphasis mine; note this word—it is key] nibbling at the table of the world. It is not the X-rated video, [because by that time one is on her way to ruin] but the prime-time dribble of triviality we drink in every night. For all the ill that Satan can do, when God describes what keeps us from the banquet table of his love, it is a piece of land, a yoke of oxen" . . . the everyday things of life, which, he continues, can "replace an appetite for God himself, the idolatry is scarcely recognizable, and almost incurable."[12] Just as we are what we eat, we become what we do.

I think it is easy to see that many of us have a serious misunderstanding of the word *leisure* corrected by looking at its etymological derivation. In Greek the term for leisure is *skole* and in Latin *skola*—from which we get our word "school." Seen this way, leisure is part of the learning process. The spirit of leisure is actually the spirit of learning, of self-cultivation. Leisure provides the venue for the growth of a person's whole being—for thinking about life's great concerns, for activities that enrich the mind, strengthen the body, and restore the soul. Like education, leisure takes discipline, training, cultivation of habits and tastes, discriminating judgments. Leisure is not something one drifts into, or one becomes a drifter; if one "veges" too much as the popular expression goes, one surely will become a vegetable. The God who ordained rest, who commanded a day of rest, cares about what we do with *all* our time.

POPULAR VERSUS TRADITIONAL

How much of what you choose to do with technology, the books you read, the television programs or movies you watch is part of popular culture, and how much is part of a classic tradition? Maybe it would be helpful to define the difference between popular culture and traditional or classic cultural thought and behavior patterns. These are standard definitions adapted from a list in Marva Dawn's book mentioned earlier.

POPULAR CULTURE	TRADITIONAL/FOLK CULTURE
1. Focuses on the new/recent	1. Focuses on the timeless
2. Discourages reflection	2. Encourages reflection
3. Pursued to kill time aimlessly	3. Pursued thoughtfully
4. Gives us what we want/tells us what we know	4. Offers us what we could not have imagined
5. Relies on instant comprehension	5. Requires training; encourages patience
6. Celebrates fame	6. Celebrates giftedness
7. Appeals to sentimentality	7. Appeals to deeper, mature emotions
8. Market-driven	8. Content and form governed by the timeless
9. Leaves us where it found us	9. Transforms our sensibilities
10. Incapable of deep, sustained attention	10. Capable of repeated, sustained attention[13]

Popular culture, wrote Douglas Wilson, "is a disposable culture for those who agree to consume it." You can't look at these lists for long before you realize that if you immerse yourselves in popular culture at the expense of traditional or classic culture, you will grow impatient with anything more demanding, you will be a superficial thinker lost in the tyrannical, ever-changing demands of whatever is "now." As I said before, it doesn't matter how much you attend Bible studies, do ministry in the church or outside the church; if the rest of your life is devoted to the passing diversions your age group or cultural setting encourages, you'll not become a woman of detailed moral sensibility, a woman who knows and practices good theology with a developing intellect, a woman who takes herself seriously and is ready to face life with clearheaded integrity. You will be a slave to every trend that comes along. That's bondage.

Let me illustrate the difference between popular and classic by looking at two movies, one of the most popular genres of our age. The two movies in question are *Titanic* and the much older *Casablanca*, a cult classic still popular in groups of all ages (its poster often hangs in coffee shops and bookstores). I chose *Titanic* because though it was made a decade and a half ago, when it came out in 1997, it hit a raw nerve. It still appears on television often and was recently released in 3-D. People flocked to the movie, all ages of people, but especially the young, many of whom were reported to have gone more than a dozen times. Also, the movie contains many of the popular, people-pleasing ingredients guaranteed to get an audience.

A great deal of money was spent making this movie; it is glitzy, the cinematography lush, the music big and beautiful, the footage from the old *Titanic* fascinating, the treatment of the breakup of the ship riveting. And the true story it is based on continues to capture the imagination of the public as seen in the traveling exhibit full of artifacts from the actual ship. The movie had the potential to be classic as a whole, not just in parts, to fit the criteria of true and lasting greatness. It could have told the stories of the unusual and well-known personalities who perished on the ship and explored suffering in a rich and universal way.

Instead, it was a great icon of popular culture and postmodern life. If we identify with the core "love" story and find it compelling, we must be honest about our motivation. It may mean that we resonate with beautiful people; that we are straining to get away from obligation as the protagonists, Rose, played by Kate Winslet, and Jack, played by Leonardo DiCaprio, are. It may mean that sexual love is a primary interest for us as in the movie it is elevated beyond any other concern and worth any risk (i.e., the couple has sex in an onboard car after a very short acquaintance; they have a relationship conversation while chained to a pipe and needing to be freed in order not to drown).

As a screenplay, the central story line violates many standards of good writing. The love story is predictable; two young, rebellious teenagers meet, fall "in heat," and connect primarily on a sexual level. The villain is ludicrous—the makeup artist overdid the eyebrows—he walks around sneering at and menacing everyone. Why did Rose hook up with him in the first place? The dialogue is often a bit silly, and how many times have we seen keys drop into the water when the character needs them, doors refuse to open, and passageways fill up with water just as the heroine brushes through, wearing, of course, a transparent dress? Finally, few women would be able to live their lives sustained by the memory of one weekend or tell her granddaughter about an illicit love affair as Rose does.

Casablanca, a much older movie, is a classic, unpredictable story of great love and heroism. Rick, played by Humphrey Bogart, and Ilsa, played by Ingrid Bergman, great actors of their time, meet in France and fall deeply in love. Ilsa is married to a hero working in the resistance movement helping those endangered by the Nazis to escape. Thinking he is dead when she meets Rick, they plan to escape the country together. Then, she learns her husband is still alive, and she does not come to the appointed meeting place. Some time later, Ilsa and her husband come to Casablanca as refugees where she meets Rick again at a popular bar he owns. The intense love between them has not died. Both of them are filled with pain though Rick is angry, not knowing that she was married or the reasons she failed to meet him. In a series of encounters, the audience watches them strain painfully toward each other, acknowledging their love and difficult circumstances. Though she respects her husband, Ilsa is tempted to be with Rick. However, in a final, very famous scene, Rick rejects that possibility. He respects the husband's heroic goodness and sacrificial efforts in the war too much to hurt him in this way. Standing in the rain as he is about to help them escape the country, Bogart says to Bergman something like "surely there must be something more important in the world than the way two people feel about each other."

This is not sentimental or predictable; furthermore it is principled. Both people, particularly the man, have transcended their deep love (not just sexual attraction) for each other to do the right thing, to honor marriage and goodness, something seldom seen in the movies. The dialogue is not clichéd. Instant gratification is thwarted not encouraged. The movie calls us to something besides hormones and feelings.

In summary, the popular form relies on instant comprehension and shallow emotion (why there must always be a new group and a new book) while the classic form requires attention and encourages patience. If we're going to be *in* this world but not *of* it, we have to understand the culture we live in while resisting its worst obsessions and idolatries. That doesn't mean we dismiss the present culture; instead we acknowledge that it can begin to form our ways of living and thinking. What I am suggesting to you today is that you remember the best of what was and include that best with the best of what is, or you will break the link in a historical legacy given to us by God. This means that popular culture can have a thoughtful place in your life, but should not dominate you by the very definition of popular. This means that it would serve you well to have at least as a portion of your experience the classics in music, art, theology, and literature—those things that have been with us for generations. That understanding will then help you look at today's music, art, and literature critically, helping you to choose and enjoy the best of it. Having gone through the process of changing your diet, you will find yourself unable to go back to junk food.

A FEW SUGGESTIONS

What I am not here to do is to ask you to dismiss all the things you do and value. What I am asking is that you refuse to give in to the postmodern notion that what is new or what you feel at the moment is better and that history or what you ought to feel and like is irrelevant. What if I had gotten stuck on "Do Lord" and "Johnny Angel"?

In the interest of being practical, here are a few suggestions for getting started in the business of being a guardian of the gate and of expanding the horizon of your experience and understanding.

1. Do a media fast with a view to figuring out how much it controls you.

2. When you're done, control your cell phone, Facebooking, and computer use.

3. Read a great hymn for devotions and think about the language, unravel the images.

4. Make it a point to watch a classic movie like *Casablanca*, or a version of *Pride and Prejudice* for example, movies encouraging restraint and moral character, or *To Kill a Mockingbird* with its magnificent antiracism speech by Gregory Peck.

5. Buy a collection of classical music themes from the movies and listen reflectively.

6. Go to an art gallery and look around until you find something that interests you. Study the painting, then do a little research on it.

7. Read a classic novel—a small list is provided at the end of this book.

8. Study the lyrics of your favorite contemporary groups, Christian or non-Christian. Is it good poetry, written in fresh images, not clichés, or just another "Do Lord" or "Johnny Angel"? Does it contain good theology, or is it just a me, me song?

What I am pleading with you to do is to remember, to become at your age, a guardian of the souls of those who follow you, to be a Keeper at the Gate so that your children and their children will still have the best of what was, will know their history, an iron thread sewn through the passing trends of the day. To go back to the theme of this book . . . so that you will be Christian women whose dignity and resolution protect you and make you a light to those around you.

SUGGESTED READING

- FICTION: *A Tree Grows in Brooklyn* by Betty Smith (a young girl finds healing and comfort in great reading); *The House of Mirth* by Edith Wharton (by contrast, the main character destroys herself through compromising herself for all the wrong reasons).

- NONFICTION: *Windows of the Soul: Experiencing God in New Ways* by Ken Gire. (This small, readable book uses literature, art, music, poetry, and prayers to create windows into one's spiritual life.)

CHAPTER 7

READING AS A SPIRITUAL EXERCISE

BY ROSALIE DE ROSSET

ROMANCE: 1a. A long medieval narrative in prose or verse telling of the adventures of chivalric heroes. b. A long, fictitious tale of heroes and extraordinary or mysterious events. 2. A novel, story or film dealing with a love affair. 3. The class or style of fictional works about idealized love.

IMAGINATION: 1. The power of the mind to form a mental image or concept of something that is not real or present. Such power of the mind used creatively. 2. The ability to confront and deal with reality by using the creative power of the mind; resourcefulness.[1]

For all their cultural value, the classics function not simply as great
books but as something closer to spiritual exercises. . . .
Taken in and savored, they become a way of understanding
oneself in relation to larger powers of the human soul.[2]

LOUISE COWAN

POPULAR LITERATURE

When I was a girl living in Peru, reading was a source of entertainment, and I read everything in sight. I and my siblings
learned to love books from my mother who read energetically from
King Arthur and His Knights, *Robin Hood and His Merry Men*, *Pilgrim's Progress*, and other literary classics, a fact which has a great
deal to do with the endurance of my Christian faith, my respect
for language, and for any success I may have. But, I was sometimes
less discriminating. I had to learn to play the piano, but because we
couldn't afford to own one, I biked to another missionary's house
to practice. He was a middle-aged widower who owned all sixty of
a series of religious, formula novels for women, whose author shall
remain nameless. By the time I was eleven, I had read them all, all
titled something like *The Color of Moonlight* or *Roses in the Sunset*.
In each novel appeared a rich hero and an impoverished heroine
or vice versa. One was regenerate, the other pagan. I remember
the poor, regenerate heroines best—they were more poetic—they
needed to be rescued.

A typical scenario reads as follows. The heroine has been left
alone by some vague disaster that has wiped out every relative to

the level of third cousin. Important to note is that she was once rich, the only way to be refined and lovely. She is condemned to live in a tenement house that smells of cabbage and ham on the wrong side of the tracks. Much like my neighborhood, I might add. She has a tiny room at the top of the stairs with a small oak bed, a wash-stand, and "tidy but tattered" curtains.

At this moment, our hero, Lance Warwick, enters the scene, driving along in his red roadster.

Our heroine, whose name is always something like Elizabeth Livingston, is drop-dead gorgeous. She weighs about 103 pounds dripping wet, has translucent skin delicately flushed with pink, wide luminous eyes in azure green or sky-blue or warm brown, and hair in such abundance and shining waves of gold or chestnut brown it is a wonder her tiny frame can hold it up. Her neck is right out of the Song of Solomon. The big hair is unaffected by her present, poor diet. Her wardrobe consists of four gingham dresses: yellow, pink, green, and blue.

Elizabeth must work, so she has found a job at the local, what we used to call a nickel and dime store, selling buttons and bows behind the notions counter. Her colleagues, as I recall, give her sal-tine crackers and oranges on which she subsists since she cannot afford the cabbage and ham of which her tenement house smells. One day as she is walking home, carrying her brown paper sack of crackers, she faints dead away from hunger. She does not fall into a dumpy heap as most of us would. Instead, she drifts onto the concrete, and her hair washes around her in a "shining veil of color." She lies there looking like a vision.

At this moment, our hero, Lance Warwick, enters the scene, driving along in his red roadster. I always wondered what he was doing on the wrong side of the tracks. Lance has been dating a hussy who has "bobbed hair" and eats bonbons. He glances over, and instead of driving by as he would for most of us, he stops and leaps out of his car. Running to the inert vision, he picks her up, which he can do without double-herniating himself because, you guessed it, she only weighs 103 pounds, dripping wet. Then he whisks her off to his seaside cottage where he nurses her back to health (all properly chaperoned). The hussy is never heard of again, her unregenerate soul apparently not a worry. When Elizabeth is still wan but lovely, she and Lance walk along the beach with their toes in the tide, and she finally speaks (the novels are not notable for the protagonists' intellectual acumen), and she evangelizes him. I don't remember what she says. Not the point I guess. Perfect man and woman marry and bear beautiful children, and bushel loads of roses climb their picket fences.

This was not classic, literary fiction; it did not use great language, deal with the complexity of what it means to be human in a fallen world, delight the senses, engage the intellect, or interpret life and motivation. This was commercial, i.e., popular fiction, stories catering to cliché and superficial emotion, aimed at a feel-good, sentimental response with little attention to language, character, or anything but plot—what's going to happen next? And they misrepresented biblical teaching, not to mention underestimating women. The effect on me, thankfully, was fairly innocuous because of my mother's watchful eye and my immersion in better books.

I knew theoretically these novels were shallow. I also realized that since I didn't have translucent skin, an ivory neck, or wide luminous eyes, the dime store people would not have given me food. Lance would not have stopped for me. I would have starved to death single and unloved, especially given Elizabeth's lack of ambition. Elizabeth Livingston was not Elizabeth Bennet or Jane Eyre, to put it mildly. Still, secretly, I hoped for good hair and the guy, saved my money for hair thickening formulas, and watched out my window for red roadsters. I spent far too much time wishing to turn a corner into perfect bliss, a pursuit destined to fail and leave me choking on broken dreams. Today, with the options presented by technology for online connecting and dating services, the time spent chasing such cotton-candy dreams has probably increased incrementally among those reading such empty stories.

In contrast, great fiction with its universal themes transcending time and place, with its elegant language and believable characters marked my choices in specific ways, heightened my imagination, filled me with longing for things bigger than myself, and ultimately, along with Scripture, gave my theology and Christian experience a backbone.

THE PERSUASIVE POWER OF GOOD READING

As noted earlier, our knowledge of God (theology) involves our minds and also includes the way our bodies sense, the way our spirits feel, as well as the way our minds reason. If the senses and emotions are not redeemed, we will become ghostly. Just as you are what you eat, you are what you read, which is why I decided to spend a whole chapter on the subject. And before I begin, I want to establish the importance of reading because people are not reading. As I wrote earlier, the misuse of technology and the distractions filling our leisure have displaced reading. As Gene Edward Veith writes so aptly, "The habit of reading is absolutely critical today, particularly for Christians. . . . Christians must continue to be people of the Word."[3]

Truth is always from God no matter where you find it.

I used to see people reading everywhere. Now, people in airports, on buses, trains, and in waiting rooms no longer read as much as they text. Even on airplanes, the minute permission is given, out come the netbooks or DVD players. Hardly a seating area exists anywhere without an enormous television dominating the space, almost always chattering, making it hard to concentrate. And how often, even in church and in college chapels, I see people texting during the sacred reading of Scripture, the preaching of the text, and prayer, an act I am convinced is a form of blasphemy, not to mention bad manners, both of which are going unaddressed in sermons.

Michael Flaherty, cofounder and president of Walden Media, notes that for the first time in modern history less than half of the adult population now reads literature (the good stuff). While the decline in reading crosses boundaries of race, education, and age, it is most evident among young adults, your age group, once the group most likely to read literature. I was surprised at what Flaherty said next. "Literary readers are more than twice as likely as non-literary readers to perform volunteer and charity work, nearly three times as likely to attend performing arts events, and nearly four times as likely to visit art museums."[4] Something about reading literary classics, old or new, with wonderful language and dimensional characterization enriches people's lives and can make them more engaged. At the current rate of loss, Flaherty points out, literary reading as a leisure activity will disappear in half a century.

In the many years I have been teaching and speaking, it appears that the average evangelical Christian is more likely to read the latest popular Christian living, how-to, or devotional book than to read a work of fiction. And when reading better books, he or she is more likely to read a good work of nonfiction than a classic novel. While I understand the importance of reading the best of both, I am particularly interested in fiction because it is not taken seriously one way or the other although its power to delight and corrupt is hard to exaggerate. As a teacher of literary novels, short stories, drama, and poetry, I know the resistance I often meet in my students. Lumping all kinds of fiction together, students argue that it is not as important as nonfiction; it does not have theological value; it's "fake," "made up," "a lie," "a waste of time," the last of which statements I find amusing as I hear about computer gaming, Facebooking, movie watching, and Internet overuse.

Then, there is the problem of whether or not the novel is written by a Christian. Truth is always from God no matter where you find it. Gifted writers, whether professing faith or not, understand and use language well, have the ability to draw realistic characters, show the complexity of earthly life, and tell the truth about their worldview. Ungifted Christian writers may distort truth and encourage poor values as seen in my example at the beginning. It is beyond the purposes of this discussion to defend this point; excellent defenses of fiction and guides to reading are available.[5]

Just as "a spoonful of sugar helps the medicine go down," Mary Poppins's famous words, so too a story can affect you more deeply than facts or propositions because it can charm you, delight you, scare you, altogether bring you into itself. Just as the Gospels show the life of Christ instead of talking about it, so too great stories show instead of telling. I could tell true accounts all day about the way literature has helped students, friends, and me comprehend a biblical concept in a new way, brought conviction and terror over the possible consequences of certain behaviors, and shown the selfishness of the way we love. I could also describe for hours the refreshment to my dry spirit an evocative novel has brought me, how let down I have felt at the end when the great pleasure of being inside a drama is over.

And, as already discussed, it is what we do in our leisure that has the greatest effect on us. The fiction we read can affect our attitudes toward others and ourselves. It is no accident that the Bible contains so much narrative. To be a thinking and dignified being, you must have a relationship to good books, to language, to the reflection those demand. How else will you be able to read Scripture with any understanding or interest? I'm often puzzled that so few of those who preach and/or talk seriously about the importance of devotions, reading the Bible and Bible study, show so little interest in great literature, and in doing so waste a rich resource.

C. S. Lewis understood the problem well. In fact, in his later years he came to believe fiction had more power to persuade than apologetics. He begins *The Voyage of the Dawn Treader*, part of the Narnia series, by introducing a new character, Eustace Clarence Scrubbs. Lewis indicates that the best way for the reader to understand Eustace is to know the kinds of books he reads. Lewis writes,

"He liked books if they were books of information."[6] In other words, Eustace doesn't have time for imaginative stories about heroism, knights, and talking animals. As a result, Eustace is at a significant disadvantage when he arrives in Narnia and finds himself in a dragon's lair. "Most of us know what we should expect to find in a dragon's lair," writes the narrator, "but as I said before, Eustace had read only the wrong books. They had a lot to say about exports and imports and governments and drains, but they were weak on dragons."[7] By reading only factual things, Eustace has starved his imagination.

In an article called "Reading Can Be Dangerous," the late Mike Yaconelli, former editor of *The Wittenberg Door*, comments that the religious book market "has become a glut of slick, simplistic 'best sellers' . . . lowered to the level of conversation pieces, status symbols and instant problem solvers." The books that keep ending up on the bestseller list are as follows: Celebrity books, Formula (how-to) Books, "Fad Books (a certain group of established religious authors develop a following and when a new fad appears, they all end up writing a book on the fad)," and Sequel Books, usually rehashes of the first book.[8]

THE ROMANCE NOVEL

We have to read to begin with, but we also have to read well. Good fiction is a wellspring of delight once we have broken the habit of consuming junk. In a wry description, T. S. Eliot writes, "The heroine of current fiction has no soul—she has not even a heart; she only has a nervous system. She has no spiritual crisis; she has only nervous reactions. Experiences which would have made the whole life of Jane Eyre . . . which would have raised her to rapture or cast her into the nethermost hell . . . our modern heroine goes through these in a week without batting an eyelid."[9] Women's intellectual junk food is often this kind of romantic fiction. The stories I read as a girl were early Christian romance novels, a genre which has exploded into a huge industry paralleling the success of the secular romance. In a web-based survey commissioned by the Romance Writers of America in May 2009, it is reported that the core of the romance fiction market was twenty-nine million *regular* readers; 24.6 percent of all Americans read a romance novel in 2008, versus 21.8 percent in 2005; 29 percent of Americans over the age of 13 read a romance novel in 2008; and women, particularly ages 31–49, make up 90.5 percent of the romance novel readership.[10]

The official definition of the romance novel is that it have "an emotionally satisfying and optimistic ending . . . the lovers who risk and struggle for each other and their relationship are rewarded with emotional justice and unconditional love." Romance novels are generic in style and setting, and "have varying levels of sensuality— ranging from sweet to extremely hot."[11] Writing about the Harlequin romance, Ann Barr Snitow, who, among other critics, calls this genre "women's pornography [air-brushed plots and characters]," delineates additional ingredients one can expect.

> The heroine is alone and . . . also gets her man at the end (this is a code for no premarital sex) and . . . the hero gets ample opportunity to see her perform well in a number of female helping roles . . . passionate motherliness, good cooking, patience in adversity, efficient planning, and a good clothes sense, though these are skills and emotional capacities produced in emergencies, and are not, as in real life, a part of an invisible, glamourless work routine.[12]

In addition, says Snitow, these heroines are generic with "no particularized character traits; . . . fit[ting] in comfortably with the lifestyle of the strong-willed heroes be they doctors, lawyers, or marine biologists doing experiments on tropical islands."[13] I once saw a large bin of books in a big box store, all small and white with one of three words written on the cover in black letters: *Mystery, Romance, Western.* That says it all.

Janice Radway, who has written extensively on women reading romances, studied twenty "ideal romances." By the end, she says, "the heroine is always tenderly enfolded in the hero's embrace and the reader is permitted to identify with her as she is gently caressed, carefully protected, and verbally praised with words of love." Radway concludes that "passivity . . . is at the heart of the romance-reading experience." Bestselling authors know that what the reader wants is man and woman in a "perfect union in which the ideal male, who is masculine and strong, yet nurturing," finally recognizes how much the heroine is worth to him.[14] Once again, the reader is looking for her heaven on earth.

A more adult version of the romance novel also exists, tales described as "bodice rippers" or "spicy" or "erotic" by the industry and also written to a formula. They include, on a continuum, explicit sexual details and constitute a huge industry. The *Twilight* series and the films that have followed, wildly popular among young girls and women and disturbing for many reasons, also fit into the romance genre with the addition of the vampire motif. Carol Falkenstein, literature professor, analyzes the darkness of the series from a theological standpoint. I mention these books because I know so many Christian young women who having read them are unable to discern their dangers, more proof of the gap between belief (what we do for God) and practice (what we do for fun), a concession to a slothful way of life discussed earlier. What these novels do, says Falkenstein, is promote idolatry.

> In *Twilight*, Genesis (the story of what happened *in the beginning*) is being rewritten. One *can* live forever, in one's youthful perfection . . . as a vampire . . . so long as one is a good vampire who resists the temptation to kill humans. No death, no sin, an Eden occupied by one vampire Adam (Edward) and one vampire Eve (Bella), and hopefully enough large animals whose blood they can drink. Bella envisages this "life" as the prelapsarian time-free, aging-free, death-free romp through the garden that existed before the fateful apple was consumed. God is out of the picture; instead, a passionate male-female love is enthroned as supreme. And to get there . . . all you have to do is *choose*. If only real life were so easy.[15]

The only notable difference between secular romances and most Christian romance titles is that the latter don't tend to venture into "hotness" except by implication, and they include a Christian emphasis or witness. Otherwise, it's business as usual. The unsaved or backslidden hero or heroine gets saved; hard things happen, people fail, but eventually all is well. It's what I call the "Jesus fixes everything" syndrome. And, as I always say when I'm talking about this, at some point the hero and heroine's "lips cling together in a heady ecstasy that knows no time," a caption I once saw in a magazine at a doctor's office. It's the fairy-tale ending without any of the imagination of a good fairy tale. Look at the definition at the beginning of this chapter. The true use of imagination asks you "to confront and deal with reality by using the creative power of the mind"; it asks you to be resourceful. These novels push you into wishful thinking, making you lazy emotionally, spiritually, and intellectually, not to mention dissatisfied with the average life you may be leading. You are then set up for failure, even moral failure.

Love in the romantic sense may just be one of the most potent weapons in Satan's arsenal.

It had been years since I'd read a romance until a national contest asked me to be a judge in the category of contemporary Christian fiction. Curious, even slightly hopeful, I agreed, and in three months read twenty-nine novels (talk about quick-read). Though the plots were more varied than those described above, some even containing hard dilemmas and potentially interesting characters, in most of them, somewhere, somehow the same romantic and spiritual clichés emerged. With the exception of a handful which had strengths and were winners, most authors, their theology seriously flawed, had Jesus fix everything quickly. It was like watching a bad magic show, embarrassing when it wasn't exasperating. Villains were punished, characters changed their ways overnight, marriage was inevitable and happy; wayward children returned to successful lives; everyone learned lessons without too many scars. There's that heaven-on-earth thing again. Love in the romantic sense may just be one of the most potent weapons in Satan's arsenal, says Paul deParrie in *Romanced to Death*. Romanticism today, he continues, is an entire philosophy built on the victory of feeling over fact, the belief that people's emotions can be trusted as guides. However, this romanticism should not be confused with the real Romance (discussed in an earlier chapter) which originally meant the glorification of ideals such as love, courage, and loyalty.[16]

The chances that many of you have read one or more of these novels are substantial; some of you read them often as I hear from the women I teach and speak to. Writing on the subject, Susan Verstraete notes that at least "one major Christian bookseller has over 2,000 current titles listed in this category." And, she adds, "There are several clubs that send members a new Christian romance novel every week." As if that's not enough, "you can surf to an author fan site or one of dozens of sites that review and suggest books in this genre."[17] I'm reminded of something a speaker said once when talking about some Christian publishers that have clearly put money above principle: "Don't be fooled—it's 'The Lord is my product; I shall not want' syndrome."

WHY WOMEN READ ROMANCES

Why do women read these books? Why do you read these books? I know why I did, and Radway's report after having done interviews with one community of romance readers confirms the truth I suspected. The stories make them feel good. They liked "stories that take your mind off everyday matters." That were "different than everyday life . . . because it is an escape and we can dream. And pretend that it is our life." Over and over the same theme came through—escape from their lives. These reasons sound like the words an addict uses to defend her drug of choice.[18] Escape here must be distinguished from the adventure of a great book which both captivates and enriches.

When researchers asked why *Christian* women read Christian romance, they answered "overwhelmingly" that "they inspired an emotional response."[19] One has to wonder about the depth of this emotion or about how much women are desperate for outlets given the predictability of the books. Verstraete, who read a lot of these, asks hard personal questions, all of which I have asked. If you read these books, have you turned off your intellect? Are you being idolatrous, giving a man the power of circumstantial salvation that belongs only to God? Is this reading changing your expectations of life? Are you subscribing to the illusion of happily-ever-after, one that will crash and burn? Are these stories leading you to believe that Jesus fixes every detail of your life instead of using the hardships of life to learn from Him? If you are married, are you committing emotional adultery? Have you developed an addiction to emotional escapism?

In a personal testimony to the dangers of such reading, Crystal Rae Nelson writes a column of caution. At eleven, she read her first Christian romance novel by a prominent name in the genre. She became "captivated," reading them by the hour, wrapped in them, her mind filled with romantic fantasies. Though her parents issued warnings, she rationalized the habit because, she says, "these stories were founded on strong Christian values . . . there was no physical immorality, . . . virtue and purity were upheld and encouraged throughout." She concludes, "I was actually benefiting from absorbing these idealistic examples of what 'falling in love' should be like." A few years later, she realized she had "misshaped" her convictions and "distorted [her] idea of a courtship."[20]

MADAME BOVARY
Emma Bovary's story in the nineteenth century classic *Madame Bovary* by Gustave Flaubert is a chilling reminder of this danger.

Emma is charmed by the wrong kind of "books that injected the first poison in her soul," writes one critic. Her reading sets her up to feel that Pascal's God-shaped vacuum is a man-shaped vacuum. She is possessed by a "contentless longing."[21] After marrying someone who cannot live up to her romantic expectations, she tries "to find out what one meant exactly in life by the words *bliss*, *passion*, *ecstasy*, that had seemed to her so beautiful in books." Often bored, she "devours" the stories in women's magazines, "all the accounts of first nights, races and soirees,[22] of the debut of a singer, the opening of a new shop. She knew the latest fashions, the addresses of the best tailors." Gradually, in her misplaced longing and boredom, her spirit is poisoned, and she gets moody, selfish, and mean. "She hated the divine injustice of God. She leant her head against the walls to weep; she longed for lives of adventure, for masked balls, for shameless pleasures that were bound, she thought, to initiate her to ecstasies she had not yet experienced."[23]

Many women have told me what the slippery slope of poor reading and movie-watching have led to, beginning with discontent and depression, sometimes ending in moral failure.

Having fed her appetite on what Lewis calls the witch's food, she is infected. The inevitable happens; she meets a man, becomes obsessed, neglects her child, and is "eaten up with desires, with rage, with hate" when she is not with him.[24] When she finally takes this man as a lover, she feels she is "entering upon a marvelous world where all would be passion, ecstasy, delirium. She felt herself surrounded by an endless rapture." She remembers then the "heroines of the books that she had read . . . adulterous women began to sing in her memory with the voice of sisters that charmed her. She became herself, as it were, an actual part of these lyrical imaginings; at long last, as she saw herself among those lovers she had so envied, she fulfilled the love-dream of her youth. . . . She tasted it without remorse, without anxiety, without concern."[25] There is no good ending for a woman so caught up in romantic illusion. Emma kills her conscience and becomes a ghost.

This story is not far-fetched. Many women have told me what the slippery slope of poor reading and movie-watching have led to, beginning with discontent and depression, sometimes ending in moral failure. Ironically, Madame Bovary's story, told powerfully by Flaubert, is far more theologically sound and truth-telling, not to mention literary, than the conventional Christian romance novel. As Madeleine L'Engle once wrote, "Where language is weak, theology is weakened."[26] I would add, where language is strong, theology may be strengthened.

I go back to the place where I started, to Jane Eyre and Elizabeth Bennet, characters in novels containing great romantic elements, even happy endings, but which present the reader not with passive heroines, easy solutions, or clichéd language. These characters do not betray their convictions; they are not sentimentalists. These heroines are "formidably self-possessed young women with detailed moral sensibilities," women who take themselves and are taken seriously. These women have restraint over their longings; they are not divided selves. They don't just respond; they *decide* what to do with their lives, every part of them.

As women, we may not think of repenting of what we read and

watch in the same way men are urged to repent of viewing pornography. However, just as pornography is an escape, a numbing of the spirit, an unrelational, solitary obsession with a digital mistress, so too, the habitual consumption of popular romances, escape fiction, or their movie equivalents can be an addiction that walls you off from yourself and the dignified, true, principled life God wants you to live.

Anne Bradstreet, the first published poet, male or female, to come from an early American heritage, became, in one biographer's words, "an electrifying personality," her small volume of poetry a runaway bestseller. While going through all the severe hardships of frontier wife and mother, she was also a rebel, "flouting the image of seventeenth-century women as too intellectually weak to tackle the male" disciplines, especially poetry.[27] Deeply spiritually motivated, she writes in "Meditation 70" that the certainty of knowing eternity lies ahead of us "should make us so number our days as to apply our hearts to wisdom, that when we are put out of these houses of clay we may be sure of an everlasting habitation that fades not away."[28]

DISCUSSION QUESTIONS

1. How much do you read? Fiction? Nonfiction? Do an inventory of your reading, listing the specific titles from the last few years.

2. What category does this reading fall into—popular or classic? What genre? Inspirational, Romance, Mystery?

3. How do you think about reading as a Christian, and where have your ideas come from? Has this chapter provoked you to think differently?

4. Set up a reading program for the next year, emphasizing classic or literary fiction. Form a club to help you.

READING SUGGESTIONS

- FICTION: *Madame Bovary* by Gustave Flaubert.

- NONFICTION: *Lit!: A Christian Guide to Reading Books* by Tony Reinke.

CHAPTER 8

SEXUAL DIGNITY
Not by Accident

BY LINDA HAINES

CHASTITY: 1. The state or quality of being chaste or pure. 2. Virginity. 3. Virtuousness. 4. Celibacy[1]

The passions may rage furiously, like true heathens, as they are; and the desires
may imagine all sorts of vain things. . . . Strong wind, earthquake-shock,
and fire may pass by: but I shall follow the guiding of that still small voice
which interprets the dictates of conscience.[2]

JANE EYRE

For you were bought with a price. So glorify God in your body.

1 CORINTHIANS 6:20

ASSESSING THE REALITIES

I go in and out of a lifestyle of drinking and sleeping with guys,"
said a female client in her first session with me some years ago.
She was in her early twenties. "And I feel numb," she added. More
recently, another young woman hadn't reached numbness yet but
wept frequently as she talked of her compulsive sexual behavior,
knowing she was violating her moral beliefs. These were not the
first occasions on which I would hear such admissions, nor the last.
Each revelation came from a professing Christian who cared about
her faith. Some who "confessed" admitted not feeling badly and
wondered why not.

In a much-quoted line, C. S. Lewis says the obvious, which is
where we must begin: "Chastity is the most unpopular of the Christian virtues." Nevertheless, chastity is the Christian rule which, he
continues, means "either marriage, with complete faithfulness to
your partner, or else total abstinence."[3] Total abstinence? That's an
uncompromising principle. Are we sure that applies to us today?
Is there any payoff here, you might ask? Yes, there is. Dignity. The

bottom line is that chastity, while first of all God's standard, is really about dignified sexual behavior.

Drawing on a wealth of survey data as well as in-depth interviews, the "surprising" reality was that "evangelical teenagers don't display just average sexual activity patterns, but rather above-average ones."

Clearly, two completely contradictory things are true about sex and today's Christian. The first is the way God has called us to live. The second is that many unmarried Christians are having sex, starting young. Surveys in the last two decades indicate the extent of the escalation in premarital sexual activity among Christians. In a fairly recent and disturbing study published under the title *Forbidden Fruit: Sex and Religion in the Lives of American Teenagers*, sociologist Mark Regnerus and fellow researchers conclude that "religion affects adolescents' sexual attitudes and motivations more than their actions." Drawing on a wealth of survey data as well as in-depth interviews, the "surprising" reality was that "evangelical teenagers don't display just average sexual activity patterns, but rather above-average ones." Even more startling are the researchers' reports on abstinence pledgers, a large number of whom are explicitly Christian. While these young people do wait a little longer to have sex than those who don't take the pledge, Regnerus reports that "the majority of pledgers do indeed break their promise somewhere on the way to the altar (and in up to 7 of 10 cases, it is not with their future spouse)."[4]

Probably any practicing Christian would give lip service to his or her understanding of God's rule of chastity, but the truth is that many of you have thought it "strange, and difficult, and curious," to quote Lauren Winner in her book *Real Sex.*[5] In a sexually charged world, sexual purity is countercultural. And what should be obvious, but often isn't, is that chastity does not happen by accident; it is a discipline of life founded on a knowledge of and belief in God's Word and His loving intent for us, supported by accountability to an insightful community. Finally, unless you pay attention to all you do, in work and play, you are likely to fail. Yet, Winner, who gives testimony to having had to learn chastity after a life of sexual license, writes that such discipline does get "easier and better with time," because it really *is* God's best for us, the best from the one who wants to protect us from objectification, who wants us to be cherished, who wants us to know the joy of living dignified, holy lives and the true joy of desire.[6] We cannot break God's rule of chastity without wounding our souls.

The realization that God's way is best and that sexual purity is an all-inclusive discipline comes far too late in the lives of many Christians. Here we are back to the problem of the divided self, back to the reality that we do take less-wild lovers who eventually devour our misplaced longing, leading us away from not only our true selves but also from God. In an exceptional book called *The Sexual Man* by Archibald Hart (a book Hart encourages men *and* women to read), he argues that "all our sexuality needs to be intimately linked with our whole personality." His wise remarks could not be phrased more incisively.

Who we are as sexual beings defines who we are as persons. Too often, however, sex and the self are kept apart—miles apart.

Many men and women have compartmentalized their sexuality in order to maintain any sense of self-respect and dignity. . . . So they keep sex separated, almost as if it is in another world. This explains why otherwise moral and upright men can have pretty sordid affairs. They have so effectively split off their sexuality that it never dawns on them that they have fractured their personalities. They lack self-integration.[7]

This is not only an apt psychological description of what the divided, unintegrated self becomes—"fractured"—but it is also completely biblical. There's that raging battle of natures again that Paul describes so well.

EVEN THEIR WOMEN

A few years ago, a tiny word in Scripture impressed upon me that, as a fairly inconsequential word, it appeared significant in its implications. The everyday word in English is *even*, an adverb. "I *even* found a pair of boots to match my outfit perfectly," one friend might say to another in discussing a new fall wardrobe for college or work. The word itself, of course, can mean different things, such as in the archaic use, "evening"; or more currently, "balanced" or "equal." The meaning I am thinking about, however, is none of these, but another, defined as, "to a degree that extends . . . used as an intensive to stress the comparative degree."[8] In my example above, the young woman who *even* found a pair of boots to match her outfit perfectly, is happier now than she was when she found the outfit.

"Even" is used often in Scripture, and perhaps a study on that alone would prove interesting. However, the verses that caught my attention were in Romans 1:25–26: "They exchanged the truth of

God for a lie, and worshiped and served created things rather than the Creator. . . . Because of this, God gave them over to shameful lusts. *Even their women* exchanged natural relations for unnatural ones" (NIV, emphasis mine). One Sunday, while teaching these verses, my senior pastor added spontaneously, "It wasn't just the boys, it was the girls too! Unclean things coming out of their mouths."[9]

The theme of this passage is that both men and women "have become filled with every kind of wickedness, evil, greed and depravity" (verse 29). However, when someone uses the word *even* with a comparative emphasis, he or she is trying to get your attention as was Paul in the book of Romans. Paul's particular message in this case is, "It's not enough that the men are doing this stuff, the women are too! This takes the problem to a new low," the apostle seems to suggest. "It can't get worse than this, can it?" Something else jumps out at me as I study this passage. Strangely, it appears that someone is expressing an expectation of women; someone presumes our goodness—more, it would appear, than it is presumed of men.

In the 2011 second trial of impeached Illinois Governor Rod Blagojevich, the all-women-but-one-man jury were said to have taken their time deliberating the case because, as I heard one newscaster opine, "Women are more ethical." Traditionally, the female sex, in general, has been thought of as the "softer" sex, which often translates into the more moral sex, i.e., they don't have the same moral proclivities as men. Think of the saying, "Behind every good man is a good woman."

Such thinking is pervasive. Some years ago, while listening to radio talk show host Dr. Laura Schlessinger in my car, I heard her angrily scolding a woman who had called in to complain about a man in her life. "It is women who are the moral gatekeepers," Dr.

Laura declared. I immediately thought of the passage in Ephesians 5:25–27 where Paul urges husbands to sacrificially "love [their] wives, as Christ loved the church" in order to "sanctify [them] . . . that [they] might be holy and without blemish." Maybe I reflected, I needed to go home and reread the verses more carefully. Who is guarding whose morals, I debated. And who really should be the gatekeeper?

The word on the Christian street seems to be, explicit or implicit, that it is men who "really" struggle with lust.

Further, whoever is keeper, I thought, that person or group of persons hasn't been doing a very good job lately. Because the stakes for women, perhaps as in Paul's day, are getting higher; women are treading on dangerous ground. To assert that women today are not susceptible to all the same temptations men experience is naive, let alone unbiblical. The theological reality is that all of us are sinners with the same proclivities. While the statistics may still reflect a gap between men and women, recent numbers show women's involvement with addictive behaviors rising and gaining momentum.

Historically, it was the sexual revolution of the 1960s that "attempted to normalize the pursuit of sexual satisfaction for women, particularly through the pursuit of premarital and multiple partners," writes Lisa Graham McMinn in her book *Growing Strong Daughters*.[10] McMinn is right that the 1960s set a precedent for women's sexual "freedom"—some of it inadvertently positive, I would assert, in advancing new studies about women and their legitimate sexual needs. Unfortunately, it may have also set a precedent for the trend of women becoming *only* sexual. Today's woman, including the Christian woman, has become acculturated to our, not only secularized, but also sexualized, society—in dress, in speech, in behavior and manners. Influenced by subscribing to a set of myths about their sex, they sometimes try to juggle opposing expectations. The ramifications can be costly, affecting a woman's sense of self, her esteem, and her relationships to others.

WOMEN'S SEXUALITY NOT TAKEN SERIOUSLY?

It is possible to suggest that women have more reasons than men to live with the compartmentalization Hart refers to and which, he adds, is "dangerous and not conducive to a balanced life."[11] The problem is their sexuality has seldom been seriously addressed. Over and over men's sexual complexities and appetites are talked about from the pulpit, in special seminars, and in other settings. The key word here may be *complexities*. Yet, the average book written to Christian women about temptation often fails to discuss the nuances of female sexuality with any depth. Also, though things are beginning to change a little, any discussion of women's sexuality is likely to be filtered through men's problems—for one, she as the focus of their temptation—rather than through the female perspective.

As a therapist, I hear Christian woman say they feel their sexual struggles are not thought to be as serious as men's. The word on the Christian street seems to be, explicit or implicit, that it is men who "really" struggle with lust. After all, "men are aroused by sight; women are aroused by touch," a simplistic aphorism that ignores the real differences and similarities between men and women. The assumption is that women's sexuality is not as hearty as men's. In fact, McMinn writes that "women [were] portrayed throughout much of history as the nonstimulated, unexcited but begrudgingly willing partner."[12]

Ironically, however, men are also portrayed as needing to be warned against and protected from women, sometimes just because women are built in a certain way. Men are then treated like passive creatures with little responsibility for their own sexuality, certainly not emotionally or spiritually healthy for them. One could almost suggest that men's sexuality has been taken so seriously that they have finally succumbed to the belief that they indeed cannot live chastely as reflected in the oft-heard saying, "Boys will be boys." When was the last time you heard "Girls will be girls" with reference to their sexuality?

The implication is that because women have little sexual passion or ability to be aroused, they must gingerly manage men who are out of control. Strangely, while men everywhere in evangelical circles, including churches, are told and expected to be leaders, women are given the job of sexually holding the line since it's thought easier for them to be good. Here women find themselves in a virtual catch-22; they are bad because they arouse men who must then be protected from them; yet, society expects them to lead the men morally because women are good.

Add to this dilemma the many women's seminars where workshops are aimed at them and not given for them. Bathsheba, centuries later, remains the archetypal seductive woman, a misreading of the scriptural text since there is no indication that she did anything wrong. The ubiquitous modesty talks are frequently filled with caution and blame, urging women to be modest for the sake of their Christian brothers. Seldom does anyone say with compassion, "I know it's hard in this culture, but dress modestly for the sake of your self-respect—for the sake of personal holiness—so that you are taken seriously as a thinking creature, and finally, so that you are not objectified and don't attract the wrong kind of man." Nor are women taught the theological and biblical principles of modesty, a discussion begun in this book. As a result, McMinn points out, particularly in reference to college-age women, "It is tough to be intentional and thoughtful about expressing one's sexuality appropriately when one is trying to make up the rules as one goes along."[13]

Critical choices made while one is still young can bequeath either long shadows or enduring beauty.

As women grapple with the logically invalid catch-22, they begin to believe the rules and myths assigned to them. Soon *their* struggles with lust, masturbation, and pornography—those same temptations as men's—go underground, unattended, in a way unseen. One intelligent young woman, who came to me struggling with compulsive masturbation, wrote in her journal

> I don't know how to fix my problem. I just need an outlet before I do something drastic, before I walk into a bar and sleep with the first man who shows me any attention, before I give it all up, before I walk out on my faith to find a better way to be who I am. The Christian world is not a safe place for me to express these things. I must always be on my guard. . . . I'm banging my face against the glass, and the blood is everywhere, but only I can see it.[14]

A woman's isolation and shame at believing herself the exception in her community, not to mention her feeling like a failure as a Christian, may silence her, rendering healing unlikely. Christians must come to terms with the truth that *even* their women are sexually tempted and troubled.

DISTURBING TRENDS

I recall some years ago buying my first computer and opening an email account. I felt a sense of eagerness and joy at the quickness with which I could now get in touch with my family, the easy access to research in my home, negating a trek to the library on a cold winter night. I also recall one day, as many of you will too, probably after clicking on an unknown email address with the same quickness and easy stroke, that suddenly my seventeen-inch screen was filled with an image I could hardly discern at first sight, until I realized it was an up-close and personal obscene color photo. Like many of you, of course, I was shocked and proceeded with the business of learning how to block such pornographic "invitations"—invitations I soon learned were available everywhere with only a click of the mouse—just for the asking. However, I wasn't asking. I knew by that stage of my life, how addictive "the stuff" could be and how destructive. I had learned of the thin line that separates lust and desire. On one side is joy, emanating from that higher desire that creates even more desire and more joy, as C. S. Lewis describes it, a virtual spring that never dries up. On the other side, however, lust awaits, also promising "joy" since lust contains within it desire, but keeping secret from one how fast *its* kind of joy is quenched because lust is not eternal at all. Lust lies.

Or visualize two parallel lines (lust and desire), one next to the other, so close you can hardly tell them apart, each beginning at practically the same point. Remember, lust contains within it desire. But one small slip of the draftsman, one line only an infinitesimal degree off, and the lines, once parallel, eventually move apart. This is how crucial one small choice can be. One of the titles of a novel written by C. S. Lewis's contemporary Charles Williams is *Descent into Hell*, an apt title that ironically describes the quiet, moral end of one of its main characters, Wentworth, after he makes what appears to be an insignificant but wrong professional choice just to please Pauline, a woman with whom he is obsessed.

Critical choices made while one is still young can bequeath either long shadows or enduring beauty. Yet, more and more young people appear to be chasing shadows, again women as well as men. One online site of an organization called Safe Families reports that one in three visitors to pornographic sites is now a woman; that is a solid third of these viewers. And that the number of women reported to be struggling with addiction to pornography is 17 percent. Based on my work with women today, I can't help wondering if that's not a low estimate. Even some years ago, the online newsletter, "Today's Christian Woman," reported that 34 percent of their female readers admitted to intentionally accessing Internet pornography; and that one in six, including Christian women, were addicted.[15] How much higher might these numbers be now?

In the city of Philadelphia, Harvest USA,[16] a discipleship and equipping organization dedicated to "proclaim[ing] Christ as Lord to a sexually broken world" has seen the same pattern among Christian women. Ellen Dykas, hired as the first full-time coordinator of women's ministries in 2007, reports that two-thirds of the women who come to the center are there to talk about sexual problems in areas conventionally seen as men's domain—sexual addictions of all kinds, including pornography, masturbation, and same-sex attractions.

Many of the women I counsel at a Chicago suburban community mental health center are increasingly caught up with alcohol and drugs, multiplying the odds of their involvement with many sexual partners and often with prostitution. And these are not just the homeless or less educated, but also those who have grown up on the city's wealthy North Shore. Christian young women are not exempt. Even without the numbing addiction of drugs or the benefit of growing up in good homes, they are becoming more openly involved in and addicted to sexual sins. Certainly, part of the reason for this increase is that their sexual struggles, particularly in what has become a sex-laden culture, have continued to be underestimated and ignored. The resulting gap in available studies and information on women continues to be a reality, although some attempts are finally being made to correct the omission. The challenges women face at this time have no doubt been surfacing for years within a sea of silence.

Please don't mistake what I am saying here. I am certainly not implying that women are not responsible for what they do or say. Of course, they are responsible. Ultimately, each of us will stand alone before God and give account of our behavior on earth. Returning to the question of who is the moral gatekeeper, I think most of us would agree that each of us—with God's help—is first and foremost gatekeeper to ourselves. I, to myself; and you, to yourself. Every day presents us with critical moral choices, big and small. How you and I respond determines our future joy and spiritual desire for God. Of course, we will need the help and strength of fellow believers and should draw on them for solidarity in the battles we face. A strong church community should be at the forefront of surrounding its women with loving prayer and accountability as they struggle against sexual sins, some of the more notable ones briefly discussed below. Ultimately with the church's help, these women will be given the hope of restored lives, a return to their self-respect and dignity and will become all that God created them to be.

PORNOGRAPHY

Such solidarity, as mentioned above, is necessary in a society where sex is so available, so discussed and joked about, and so susceptible to becoming habitual in the lives of those viewing pornography. The increase in women's viewing such sites is leading to addiction, just as it is for men. Another client, in her early twenties, again a Christian, sometimes wrote letters to me about her growing online addiction, since it felt easier for her than talking. In one letter she began, "I'm really sad. I've been online for hours. I'm sick with myself." And later in another, "Yesterday was a bad day. I had been fighting so long that I finally gave up and went online for a while—hours again, I'm sure." She then wrote that she had afterward taken a long hot shower which made her feel better. "But that's not right, is it?" she asked. "Shouldn't I feel a lot worse? I thought I'd wake up miserable and regretting giving in."[17] Such is the entanglement of emotions involved with addiction to pornography with its come-and-go tease of offering relief, then bringing shame and eventually numbness from the continuous cycle. Addiction leads to distorted thinking and beliefs and can make a young woman unsure of herself, erasing past confidence and opening her up to compartmentalization and denial. Certainly, this is a hotbed for the self to become divided. Any spiritual longing a Christian young woman may have initially felt in her walk with God will, in time, be stolen by this thief.

The practice of viewing pornography, like masturbation, also discussed briefly in this chapter, conditions sexuality in ways it was never intended to be practiced. It is a lonely and solitary affair, unrelational, and actually immature since it doesn't foster qualities necessary in developing trust and mutual selfless love in relating to another. Without this very human process, isolation and fantasy abound and soon may whisk you away to unreality, reinforcing your addiction. In the end, all you have is still *the chase*, ever promising, never fulfilling, never providing the love you seek. In a recent article, Reinhard Hütter, Christian theologian at Duke Divinity School, wrote, "The lust of the eyes that feeds on Internet pornography does not inflame but rather freezes the soul and heart in a cold indifference to the human dignity of others and of oneself."[18]

Each time a young woman indulges her compulsion to view pornography, she walks closer to an abyss from which there may or may not be a return.

The practice is deadly, I tell my clients. The stories of the lives, marriages, and children devastated by pornography entering their homes are told everywhere, even in the church.[19] As Alice Miller has written, "It is what we cannot see that makes us sick."[20] Even if you are minimally involved in viewing porn, you are in danger of not only hurting your life, but you also wound the emotional and spiritual life of your present or future mate and family. People with addictions—and women are no different—become steeped in lies to themselves and their families, lies that contend, "It's not that bad," "I don't do it that much," and "I can control it." When I counsel spouses or friends of those with addictions, I caution them to make sure they multiply the addict's stories, sometimes by twos, often by threes, or more. Almost without exception, the habit is worse than reported. Each time a young woman indulges her compulsion to view pornography, she walks closer to an abyss from which there may or may not be a return. Just as I warn women about becoming involved with a man who views pornography, I also warn a man if his girlfriend is involved. Pornography is an addiction that goes to the heart of the soul and spirit, carrying with it a multitude of other sins, including exploitation of others, deceit on a sophisticated level, and the waste of money, energy, and time. This less-wild lover, when chosen, is demonized with palpable evil.

If you are viewing pornography at all, seek help and account-ability, whether in counseling, in twelve-step programs, or through working with a mentor who will lovingly be ruthless with you. You may need all the above to help you out of the problem. Remember, however, it takes time for anyone with a consistent habit to heal. You may need to reconsider some of your life plans, such as waiting longer to marry, or breaking up with someone who, whether subtly or not has encouraged your habit. Be aware that pornography's root problems may lead to poor dating choices. A young woman can get caught up in either idealizing or sexualizing the relationship, con-sciously or unconsciously.

Any woman who indulges such an addiction is not ready to develop a long-term relationship leading to marriage. It has been said many times, and it still holds true: marriage does not solve one's problems, including (or especially) addiction; it only brings an unaware person into the tragedy, something he doesn't deserve. This might seem a hard line to draw, one with which some of you may disagree. However, having worked for many years with sexual and other addictions, I stand behind my words. At the same time, I also stand on the belief that God is still in the business of healing and will heal those who truly desire it.

MASTURBATION

Very little writing by Christians addresses masturbation in any detail; what is written, as might be expected, is devoted to men's concerns. Even Mark Regnerus's detailed study, cited earlier, includes only a handful of pages about the subject and admits that there is very "little data to go on." Regnerus summarizes briefly the opinions of well-known evangelicals including James Dobson and Stanton Jones who conclude that "tolerating adolescent masturbation is less harmful than its condemnation," but they also warn against "compulsive masturbation," and urge the channeling of sexual energy into more "positive outlets" such as athletics, Regnerus reports.

Others, he writes, conclude that masturbation should be avoided because of its almost inevitable connection to lust . . . because "ultimately, solo sex is not God's intention for human sexual expression."[21]

While moral issues are important to the debate about masturbation, so are psychological ones, such as the poignant reality of its use as an escape from stress or feelings of emptiness, or other out-of-control life circumstances. Nevertheless, as masturbation becomes habitual, it can create its own emptiness and become addictive. Archibald Hart describes the cycle as it might occur in the context of growing up in a religious home in which guilt about sexual feelings may initiate the process. The young adult will then resist those feelings, inadvertently causing even greater inner tension, and finally, need to seek relief. Once relieved, remorse as well as guilt and shame arise again, starting the whole process over.[22]

While perspectives vary, masturbation is not a healthy practice as it teaches that immediate gratification is part of sex and removes sex from the context of relationship rendering it an immature and lonely engagement. Finally, if it includes fantasy about someone who is not thinking about you, it may be closely linked to pornography; if the fantasy is about someone you *are* involved with, it is fornication and can lead to acting out. Fantasizing itself can be harmful for, as Lewis Smedes writes, "The more one enjoys sex with fantastic perfection, the more difficult it becomes to relate to an imperfect, real spouse." Chastity again would call us to total abstinence.[23]

The most intelligent and compassionate treatment I have read, one I recommend to the the young women who are haunted by the habit, is a small booklet called *My Beautiful Feeling*, published in 1976 and written by Walter and Ingrid Trobisch. I would encourage every woman to read it if for no other reason than to understand how to talk to those one meets who need to be heard and helped.[24]

The Trobisches decided to publish this personal correspondence when upon mentioning masturbation in an earlier booklet, the majority of letters they received were "desperate cries for help," cries that were not just coming from "a repressive education that had produced guilt" but from the post-sixties breakdown of sexual taboos. The reasoning already out there at the time that "no harm is done" did not, the couple said, "quench the subjective feeling of a shameful personal defeat. In spite of all the soothing arguments in favor of masturbation, few are really happy with it."[25]

The book contains a correspondence with a young woman, Ilona, whose letters the Trobisches chose because she was articulate and honest and also because she was not a "special case" but basically a "psychologically and physically healthy, normal girl." As an aside, some of you may be "special cases," that is those who have had early experiences of abuse, exposure to pornography, or accidental stimulation. While this booklet will still be helpful, do not be afraid of getting professional help or finding a support group in which to unravel your tangled history.

Interestingly, Ilona was afraid of one thing—that the authors might tell her what she had already heard too often: "Keep on doing it [masturbating] and stop worrying. It won't do you any harm. It might even be beneficial to your sexual development," advice that violated God's deep-seated voice in her.[26]

Allaying Ilona's fears, the Trobisches explained that masturbation is a sign of a deeper problem, not necessarily sexual but more likely "a feeling of dissatisfaction with oneself and one's life which has taken a sexual form." And, of course, the more one is dissatisfied, the more one is tempted, creating a vicious cycle. The psychological combined with biblical truth in this work, while avoiding legalism and rationalization, make this treatment of masturbation unique among other discussions. The letters show in detail the ups and downs of the struggle, the "immaturity" and self-centered "desire for pleasure" of such sexual activity, and the personal choices and life circumstances, including dating relationships and family problems that can trigger the temptation. Honesty and discipline are required of us in order to live healthy and holy Christian lives, disciplines best practiced in community with accountability.[27]

SAME-SEX ATTRACTION

A "landmark" UCLA study found that friendships between women are special, that they can shape our lives and influence our futures. They "soothe [us] . . . fill the emotional gaps in our marriage, and help us remember who we really are." Beyond that, scientists speculate that good friendships counteract daily stress . . . that brain chemicals actually cause women to befriend each other and maintain those friendships. Simply put, "friendships help us live better."[28] I could not stress more the significance of friendships to making and maintaining many of the life choices this book addresses.

> The numbers of Christian women conflicted over their sexual identities is increasing, a reality I have seen in my practice.

However, friendship, as noted by several authors,[29] is a much undervalued relationship, always coming in second to family and erotic love (eros), even though at its best friendship is the least needy, the least self-serving, and potentially invaluable to our well-being because it has greater objectivity. That being said, friendship that includes cloying dependency with or without the sin of physical involvement, attachment that is marked by emotional immaturities, crippling dependency, exclusivity, and insecurity and need is not what I would consider healthy and beneficial. God's principles affecting friendship exist for our good because such attachment is paralyzing in its addictive features, a form of idolatry keeping those who choose it in a virtual prison. God wants us free—if only we could see the beauty of that release of spirit.

Over the years I have counseled many women, both single and married, whose presenting problem is same-sex attraction. The problem touches women's lives and men's as well. Female homosexuality, again, has been given far less attention than its male counterpart. Yet, the numbers of Christian women conflicted over their sexual identities is increasing, a reality I have seen in my practice.

It is encouraging to see the recent work of professional counselor Janelle Hallman in this area of same-sex attraction. Recognizing the problem and noting significant gaps in treatment, her extensive research and work with women resulted in a comprehensive and compassionate understanding of women's dependencies and attendant behaviors. Her book, *The Heart of Female Same-Sex Attraction*, is widely praised by professionals as a necessary tool for any therapist.

Hallman writes that while there can be elements of genuine affection in same-sex attractions, she sees serious underlying problems of idealization and unresolved childhood attachment that create a barrier to healthy adult mutuality. She writes of still another kind of divided self that is often reflected in these women's confident external demeanor contrasted with the vulnerable little girl inside who just wants to be loved.

Believing as I do also that homosexuality is a part of the fall and a departure from God's design, Hallman lays out a full philosophy of treatment that leads to, in her words, "an integrated and consolidated sense of self and the capacity to psychologically and emotionally receive the presence of another without a loss of self or a dependent consumption of the other."[30] The book is an invaluable help for all adults, those who struggle and those who care for them.

NOT BY ACCIDENT

Becoming sexually healthy and obedient to God's loving rule will not happen by accident. As Archibald Hart puts it so eloquently, "The integration of our sexuality into our whole personality is painful, hard work. We have to force ourselves to be ruthlessly honest about who we are in the deep, secret corners of our sexual minds." That integration, continues Hart, will also mean being open with the appropriate person or persons who can help you. You will have to be willing to "limit the expression of some of [y]our desires," seeing and admitting your "obvious distortions" so they can be healed, and come to a "frank acceptance of [y]our basic sexual makeup."[31]

Limit[ing] the expression of some of [y]our desires will include monitoring what you do with your leisure, as stated earlier, what you read, what you listen to, what movies you see, and whom you are friends with. This process may leave a void, one you will have to fill with healthy pursuits. Changing your sexual appetite will take time, but the rewards are a life that is ultimately richer, deeper, and more satisfying. We need to consistently nurture the longing I have spoken of and are encouraged once again by the words of C. S. Lewis who wrote in *The Weight of Glory*, "Longing transforms obedience as gradually as the tide lifts a grounded ship."[32] The problem is not that we desire too much, he says, it's that we desire too little.

Finally, the community you choose to help must not be, as Winner puts it, stuck in evasions or "pretense"; it must be "a place where sin can be spoken of freely, with contrition, but without fear." She adds that "communities working toward chastity ought to have honest and true conversations about sex, conversations that include opportunities for counsel and witness."[33]

In his Sonnet #129, William Shakespeare issues a dark warning about the way lust devastates the spirit, calling it "perjured, mur-derous, bloody, full of blame/Savage, extreme, rude, cruel, not to trust." He also describes the familiar scenario sinful human beings enter into. "Mad in pursuit, and in possession so;/Had, having, and in quest to have, extreme;/ . . . Before" [they sin, it is] a joy propos'd; behind a dream [nightmare]." Shakespeare concludes ruefully, "All this the world well knows; yet none knows well/ To shun the heaven that leads men [and women] to this hell."[34]

It is incumbent upon us to remember this truth. But we need God. As Hart says so beautifully, "Frankly, without God's guidance and support and the special work of His Spirit, I doubt if we can ever successfully complete this journey toward sexual wholeness."[35]

DISCUSSION QUESTIONS

1. What are the myths you have heard and believed about women's sexuality?

2. How have these myths influenced your relationship with God?

3. What in your life (activities—movies, music, reading, Internet) might be contributing to your sexual temptation? Keep a journal of honest responses in order to analyze your profile.

4. If you are involved in sexual sin, what plan might you develop to return to total abstinence?

SUGGESTED READING

•   FICTION: "A Temple of the Holy Ghost"—a short story by Flannery O'Connor.

•   NONFICTION: *The Meaning of Sex: Christian Ethics and the Moral Life* by Dennis P. Hollinger

CHAPTER 9

A THEOLOGY OF MODESTY
Naked yet Unashamed

BY STACIE PARLEE-JOHNSON

MODESTY: Propriety in dress, speech, and conduct.[1]

Women who dress and act "modestly" conduct themselves in ways that shroud their sexuality in mystery. They live in a way that makes womanliness more a transcendent, implicit quality than a crude, explicit quality.[2]

WENDY SHALIT

Then the eyes of both were opened, and they knew that they were naked. And they sewed fig leaves together and made themselves loincloths.

GENESIS 3:7

REVEALED

I remember my wedding day. I was anxious, excited, and dressed like an elongated snowball. As a self-identified "tomboy," a T-shirt and jeans were more normal for me than high-heeled shoes and ringlets. However, on this day, I wanted to be beautiful. I wanted others to think I was beautiful too—not only my soon-to-be husband, but the other men and women watching us say our vows and don our rings. So, I dressed the part of a princess and wore pure white with buttons and pearls, a veil on my head, and earrings in my ears. My dress was strapless, and as I looked in the mirror moments before I was to say "I do," I couldn't help noticing the vast expanse of pink skin separating my necklace from the neckline of my dress. Poking out of the top of my dress, I discovered cleavage. Cleavage. Of course, I was what I imagine many Christian women long to be on their wedding day—pure, excited, and again, what I called "beautiful." This beautiful was, of course, in part "sexy." And here, in my lust to be sexy, which I wrongly equated with beauty, is where the contradiction this chapter speaks of appears—the great divide lying between modesty and practice and the reality of our lives with Christ.

The idea of a bride revealing physical nakedness on her wedding day shows a shift in Christian thinking, one that has gradually emerged as we have become more "relevant." I fear we are now so culturally entrenched that we miss the biblical understanding of what being shaped by the gospel of Jesus Christ means. Instead of our choices in dress, behavior, and speech being formed by our biblical theology, we let culture seep into our lives and mold us. We cater to the *InStyle* and other women's magazines mentality, instead of listening to the Words of Him who brought us into being. You might be thinking: How do these two seemingly unrelated pursuits go together—Christ and modesty? What does Christ have to do with what I put on or take off, with what I say or do not say? As addressed earlier by other writers, the question itself betrays the problem, the divided self rising up.

In Christ, decency in behavior and dress is far larger than the particulars of modesty.

The crux of my argument is this—we cannot truly understand what we should put on, say, or do, without looking at our behavior in relationship to Christ. In Christ, decency in behavior and dress is far larger than the particulars of modesty. By the world's standards, modesty is a rule passed down from generation to generation which involves choosing a garment that submits to a certain standard set by a mother or a community, one that constantly changes.

However, in the righteous, true, and Christian sense, modesty is a form of holiness. Perhaps the reason we view modesty so superficially is because we have succumbed to relativism and allowed our culture to define modesty for us. This is true of any rule or statute which trumps the gospel. For example, while unbelievers can be moral, they cannot be holy because they are not being conformed to Jesus Christ.

It seems possible to suggest that today's evangelicals lean on morality instead of on a foundational understanding of what it means to be in union with the Father, Son, and Holy Spirit, of what salvation means, of what the gospel does to lives. This misunderstanding directly affects how women view themselves, what they put on in the morning or choose to leave off, and how they behave inside and outside the church walls.

I am in no way positing that contemporary Christians do not think about their choices in clothing, conversation, and behavior. Lists of "what not to wear, say, and do" abound. Instead, my argument is that these boundaries seem sketchy and easily ignored because they have no foundation. A list of rules for dress is not the same as understanding *why* we put on clothes in the first place. A list of topics to be avoided in less-than-intimate conversations is not the same as understanding why some things are best kept behind closed doors. Instead, we blow wildly in the circuitous wind of fashion and fads. We let the whimsical editors of magazines, the Internet, television, and yes, even our families, guide us, because we haven't thought about modesty (understood here as holiness in dress, speech, and behavior) long enough to understand that our true guide is more omniscient than *Vogue* or Oprah. We lack understanding of *who we are in Christ*; we are vague on how that should shape every area of our lives.

COVERED

The idea of modesty is not new ground. Remember the alleged buttoned-up, tight-lipped, and three-petticoated Victorian era? I've often wondered if the modesty we attribute to the queen and her subjects isn't falsely placed. More cleavage appeared then at a ball than I've witnessed at some high school dances. Modesty then, seems to be relative. In her book *A Return to Modesty*, Wendy Shalit offers a thorough and sobering look at the cultural guidelines of the late twentieth century—where exactly society lost its modesty compass. She also makes suggestions as to how to recover that compass. While Shalit's work is among the best philosophical treatments of the subject and should be read, she sheds light on the issue of modesty from a moral, not a Christological, point of view. Her appeal to the importance of modesty stems from what it means to be feminine. She calls on women to be modest for womanhood's sake, not a bad start. One of her arguments is that modesty should be practiced partly because of men's proclivity to objectify a woman's body and make her a "thing" rather than a human being. In other words, she argues that the practice of modesty helps women be taken more seriously, certainly a good reason for practicing this "virtue."[3] However, missing at the center of her argument is Christ.

Having rules to follow is so much easier than thinking about the reasons behind the rules.

Speaking of books on modesty, a plethora of books and pamphlets authored by contemporary Christian authors are available at Christian bookstores. Their works offer important insights worthy of reflection; however, in some cases, they are incomplete. First of all, most of them are addressed to teenagers only. Of course, it is in our teens to early twenties that we first explore clothing choices and "sexuality," but not only this age group is involved in the struggle to adapt to culture or look a particular part, or the only women who feel the desire to be noticed and wanted. Usually, women of a certain age (forty-plus, for argument's sake), seem to be excluded from the conversation as if when ripe sexuality and young longing has passed, a woman no longer tries to be sexually attractive or desirable. Perhaps these writers assume that older women have arrived at a complete understanding of what it means to relate the gospel to dress. Both assumptions are critical missteps, since many older women still seek sexual fulfillment and need to be desirable— as evidenced by the annual financial records of leading cosmetics companies and their age-markets. Oil of Olay isn't catering to the youth of the nation.

A second problem with current literature on modesty is that the contents too often boil down to a list of rules. Christians love this. I love this. Having rules to follow is so much easier than thinking about the reasons behind the rules. Rules are black and white—do this, don't do that. You know your dress is too short if it doesn't meet the "three-finger rule." Three fingers between your kneecap and your dress, and you're good to go. Your shirt is too tight if you can pinch the fabric between your breasts and it bounces back to a taut fit. When we actually have to stop and think about why we do what we do, it gets complicated. The authors of these texts at times miss the "reason behind the rule." They offer some insight and are sincerely trying to help women in their pursuit of modesty. But modesty is not the first priority. Holiness is our calling as Christians.

A third problem with the existing literature is that the messages, often written by Christian women for Christian women, mix cultural relevancy with biblical truth. While these works are not without theological sensitivity, regrettably, this sensitivity focuses more often on men than on women.[4] On the many occasions when I've heard Christian speakers talk to women about modesty, the theses of their arguments revolve around a central theme—*Do not cause your brothers to stumble. Men are more visual; therefore, you need to cover up.*[5] While, true, a Christian woman should consider her Christian brothers when choosing outfits or modes of behavior, there is a higher principle. Just as using modesty as a tool for man-catching is theologically problematic, so too making men's lust the primary consideration in what one does misses the heart of the issue. Holiness and modesty *are relational*—but the relationship is not first about our Christian brothers and sisters. Instead, the relationship with the Father, Son, and Holy Spirit is primary, one that demands attention to self-respect.

Finally, by all appearances few women seem to be listening to the writing on modesty. In the end, Christian women wear, say, and do what suits them, more often than not caving in to fashion or "cultural relevancy," as if these two ideas trump their relationship with Christ and its demands. Ultimately, I fear Christian women have little grounding in biblical theology generally, as has been addressed earlier, but particularly in the area of modesty. They don't clearly understand God's message to "adorn themselves in respectable apparel, with modesty and self-control."[6] They don't understand the purpose of clothing; therefore, they cannot make wise decisions. If we don't align our clothing choices to the person of Christ, we cannot or will not make appropriate daily clothing choices. Maybe we don't understand why we say and do what we do—why we long to be desired physically and spiritually because we've never been curious. We simply act.

True nakedness in this account is more than a mere physical condition. It indicates a right relationship with God.

Where do we begin? And how do we proceed without seeming frumpy and outdated? And, to think biblically can seem clichéd— "What does the Bible say about that?" However, the Bible is where the Christian must start. I began by speaking about my wedding day—now it makes sense to go back to the first wedding, Adam and Eve's.[7]

CLOTHING'S INVENTION

In the garden of Eden a man and woman, the first of their kind, stood together in the presence of God's goodness. They smelled the fragrant air, picked fruit from the heavy laden trees, and drank from unpolluted waters—all created for them and perfectly suited to their needs. They looked at one another, and, in their pure and holy state, they "were both naked and were not ashamed."[8] Created to be companions, Adam and Eve were bent on helping, trusting, and loving one another. They had the blessing of being sure that they were intended to remain in perfect union with one another and with the Father.

The main point to consider is that they were naked and unashamed. One has to ask the question, why? I stand in front of a mirror naked, and I'm ashamed just looking at myself, let alone having someone else look at me. My shame comes from my imperfections. Did their lack of shame come from their *want* of imperfections? Some commentators argue exactly that. How can a perfect people be ashamed of themselves? The point is given credence when we look at our world, at the lack of shame among celebrities who take off their clothing and expose their bodies easily on the covers of magazines for a worldwide audience. They are "physically perfect" and, therefore, know no shame, just like the first couple.

As much as this seems reasonable, comparing God's perfect creation (naked and unashamed) with those created post-fall and living in total depravity, physically and spiritually, cannot be a correct understanding of the Genesis account. The explanation that Adam and Eve were unashamed in their naked state *because of* their bodily perfections seems shallow and insufficient at best. True nakedness in this account is more than a mere physical condition. It indicates a right relationship with God, which includes both the physical and spiritual state, a point that will be developed.

However Adam and Eve looked, we know how the beginning of their story (our story) ends. The first consequence of Adam and Eve's sin mentioned in Genesis is that "the eyes of both were opened, and they knew that they were naked. And they sewed fig leaves together and made themselves loincloths."[9] God is specific here. The direct correlation between disobedience and rebellion is shame in nakedness and the putting on of *clothing*. Nancy Leigh DeMoss points out that "from this point on in the Bible, nakedness (outside of marriage) is referred to as shameful."[10]

Why this emphasis? Why did God use nakedness and shame to show that Adam and Eve were broken in their relationship with the

Father and with one another? While it is true that the moment they failed one another and mistrusted their benevolent Father they began to die, we have no biblical basis for believing that the effects of such a death were physically immediate. In other words, they didn't cover themselves because pockets of cellulite appeared around Eve's hips or bald patches showed on Adam's brow. They didn't seem to be covering their sin *along with* their physical selves; instead, they covered their physical selves *because of* their sin. The two ideas are inseparable—spiritually they are no longer in union; therefore, physically they are also no longer in union, with one another and with God.

Adam and Eve cover themselves because the covenant with God and with one another is broken. Marriage is broken, and the security of it is torn from them. In the retelling of the first Adam story, the emphasis is often placed on the relationship between Adam and Eve. Children's picture Bibles show illustrations of the first humans behind bushes, anxious and wanting to run away. The pictures suggest they are hiding from God, yes, but they *first* seem to be covering themselves from one another. In these simplistic versions, the focus is on *their* relationship—the nakedness that they see mirrored in each other. While it is true that they cover themselves from one another because they're ashamed of themselves, the true nature of their new, devastated relationship comes from a much greater union they have broken. They ultimately cover themselves before God.

The security of the oneness they felt with the Father has been damaged, seemingly irreparably. Instead of acknowledging this, our picture Bibles and childish imaginations interpret Adam and Eve gazing at one another in shame and nakedness—heads bowed, frantically scraping together leaves, trying to mask their vulnerability from each another. Rarely is the leap made from their relationship with one another to their relationship with God. However, the latter relationship is what God addresses first. God makes a point of dealing with their lack of faith in Him—evidenced in their disobedience. Then He begins to speak of their nakedness. When God asks Adam, "Who told you that you were naked?"[11] He acknowledges that a relationship has changed—namely God's relationship with His created beings. He asks because a promise has been broken. God's command was that they not eat from the fruit of the Tree of Knowledge of Good and Evil. Seduced by Satan, Adam and Eve failed to trust God's benevolence. They broke their union with the Father and were left ashamed and revealed—physically and spiritually. The nakedness before God comes first, and then the shame of seeing one another in such a vulnerable and mistrusting state.

Adam and Eve's nakedness was so shameful that they tried to clothe themselves, again shielding themselves from one another's eyes but also from the sight of the Father. Just as all of our human efforts to cover our sins fail, so did theirs. They covered their shame with fig leaves. But this was not covering enough. The Father saw them physically and spiritually. The spiritual vulnerability led to physical vulnerability. Adam's first concern was with himself not with God, and then Eve. Eve's first concern was with herself not with God, and then Adam. Spiritually, they were now dead, which, in turn, led to their physical death.

Believers *put on*, like a garment or piece of clothing, Christ Himself.

But God's mercy is wonderful beyond measure, impossible to explain. *Through a bloody sacrifice*, He made the first clothes for Adam and Eve out of animal skins. God covered them more fully then they alone could do. God seems to say here, "You have sinned and are no longer what you should be. Let Me cover your sin with this protective shield of living sacrifice." This covering of self—a covering of nakedness—is what clothing was invented for.

CLOTHING'S PURPOSE

Understanding where clothes come from is crucial to understanding the purpose of that clothing. Clothing is a gift from God covering our nakedness and shame. Just as Adam and Eve struggled to sew fig leaves together, so too our fallen humanity struggles, apart from God, to find covering for our sin. Our efforts are unsuccessful, so God covers our shame Himself. Today, when we stand naked in our bedrooms and put on clothing, we are, in a sense, acknowledging and confessing that our relationship with God and with others is not what it was in the pre-fall garden.[12] Clothing confesses that humans are "without." We are no longer in the perfect state of wedded union and bliss God originally intended for us. Instead, we are now untrustworthy, vulnerable to one another, and lacking faith in the benevolence of God. Clothing is a confession to all of that.

Now stay with me, as this gets a little technical. Around AD 32, another Adam, the second Adam, is naked. He is shamed by man but not by God. Christ is on the cross, a bloody sacrifice, unclothed and revealed, vulnerable—just as we were in Adam in the garden. The parallel here is that when we speak of Christ's sacrifice which procures our salvation, we actually speak of clothing. This is so interesting. Clothes or lack thereof play a role in Christ's death and resurrection. First, there's Christ's nakedness on the cross though our crucifixes try to cover Him. Ironically we, a society so quick to bare ourselves, are ashamed of *His* nakedness. Christ on the cross was fully revealed, spread open in a manner truly mortifying to any human. But Christ is without clothing as He suffers and dies for our sins. This lack of clothing is integral to our understanding of Adam and Eve's nakedness. Do you see the parallel? Christ is overturning Adam and Eve's sin. He takes on their nakedness and shame and bears it Himself. Through bearing nakedness and shame, Christ becomes our righteous clothing.

Even the plainest and most rigid of us longs to be desired.

This isn't a new idea. The theological understanding of Christ as clothing can be traced throughout the New Testament: "But put on the Lord Jesus Christ, and make no provision for the flesh, to gratify its desires."[13] "For as many of you as were baptized into Christ have put on Christ."[14] Believers *put on*, like a garment or piece of clothing, Christ Himself. Christ clothes us at conversion, will continue to clothe us as we are sanctified, and at the time of righteous judgment, we will be seen through Christ in us, through our wearing of Christ. The need for clothing is a confession of our need for Christ Himself.

CLOTHING APPLIED

So then, the question remains, why, if the connection can be made from Christ to clothes and clothing can be seen as confession, is it so hard to choose what to wear? Why is it a challenge to cover up—why do we seemingly cry out for nakedness? Maybe a review would be helpful. When Adam and Eve sinned, they broke their union with God and with one another. They destroyed what God intended for them. Man's vocation was perverted from caretaker to controlling and dominating master, making manhood exploitative and selfish. True womanhood was perverted as well. In the garden we were thoughtful life-givers, nurturers, and companions. After the fall, we too may try to control and exploit men, and even other women, to placate our selfish desires. We use what we have—and it is an effective tool—for the purpose of control and manipulation. We use seduction aimed at arousing lust, usually in the form of physical nakedness, what our world calls "sexy," a gross distortion of God's intention for sex. We hear, either explicitly or implicitly, that "beauty is power," and since our understanding of beauty is often dualistic,[15] we come to believe that physical beauty is the greatest power of all. And power, well, power equals control. Are you following? Control is what every sinner wants. Control over choices, even over our salvation (the ability to earn or merit it in some way), and control over every other living being. It's hard to admit it. But it's true. This understanding of nakedness and the physical self filters into our daily routines as we stand before closets and mirrors, preparing to take on the world.[16]

Some of you will take offense at the above statements. You don't "feel" as though you want control. You don't see yourselves as using your allure to get what you want. And you certainly don't feel that the desire for control through nakedness is as pervasive as I make it out to be. However, have you ever wanted to be physically desired? Of course you have. You must ask yourself the question: How does this manifest itself? Even the plainest and most rigid of us longs to be desired. So begins the conversation about why we want to be wanted and why we choose to wear what we wear.

POWERFUL CHOICES

It must be obvious that a woman's sexuality and nakedness can entice and seduce men. Simply walk into any mall and you'll be confronted with women in sultry clothing (at times, little to no clothing at all) or a model donning a suggestive look. Sex sells and certainly we're saturated with it in our society. Some works, Christian ones at that, imply that God intended our bodies to drive men crazy and thus we must consider how we dress. Modesty is deemed a power that one can wield to attract the "right kind of man." This advice sounds more like *Cosmopolitan* magazine than the Old or New Testament ("Or do you not know that your body is a temple of the Holy Spirit within you, whom you have from God? You are not your own, for you were bought with a price. So glorify God in your body" 1 Corinthians 6:19–20). The focus of some of these popular works is that a woman's body, clothed and unclothed, is a weapon that can be used for holy purposes. If one dresses modestly and covers herself, one can brandish the power of seductive beauty and still be within the bounds of holiness.

The world, and Christians as well, seem to confuse one unholy idea (lust) with its holy counterpart (sexual desire). The Bible warns against the lust of the eyes and the lust of the flesh in 1 John 2:16, among other places. It is hard to avoid and hard to want to avoid lust, either as its object or its perpetrator. Even the great church father Augustine noted the seductive power of sexuality as he prayed, "Lord, give me chastity and continence . . . but not yet." Augustine perfectly summarizes the push and pull we feel as Christians. We want to be sexually desired, and the world shows us lust by using sex to sell a range of products from lingerie to hamburgers. Lust, however, has merely a perverted relationship to true sexual desire, which is holy and good. Lust has no place in the Christian's life. Sexual desire in the purest sense is what a man has for his wife and what a wife has for her husband. It is sexual in nature, but it doesn't objectify; it is relational; it acknowledges the fullness of a person—a wife, a human being, a follower of Christ. How is it that we have come to use these terms interchangeably, one holy and one a perversion of holiness?

In a work called *Glittering Vices*, Rebecca DeYoung defines lust as a "reductive impulse." She states that it reduces sexual pleasure (and desire) to "ones own individual gratification apart from a relationship to a person . . . [and, in turn makes] sexual pleasure [and desire] purely physical apart from its integration into our full humanity."[17] The error of mistaking lust for sexual desire directly affects how we view our nakedness (and longing to be naked). If we aim to be lusted after, we are missing the central point of sex. I cannot say it often enough—lust is not sexual desire.

We can see the distortion of desire into lust when we use our bodies to entice our "more visual" male counterparts. But I see something else in this desire, the theology in it. Here is a God-given need that's being worked out in front of our mirrors every day. For me, the question is not about how we, as women entice men with our nakedness, but about our desire to be naked in the first place. We strive to be sexually desired. And this is where we discover why dressing in a holy fashion is hard and seemingly such an anomaly in today's Christian world. Nakedness with the consequence of lust is (at times) our outlet when what we really crave is to be sexually desired. Ultimately, we are crying out for a true sexual and spiritual union. We are seeking our Adams.

As noted earlier, when God designed the garden, He created man. He realized that it was not good for man to be alone so He created woman to be his companion. They were naked, unashamed, and in perfect union with one another. When their sin destroyed this relationship, it did not annihilate God's creative intention, but it did distort it. God designed us for union, and we crave it still.

This is why we desire to be naked, because we desire intimacy. This is a comforting truth. It means that our desire to be desired and thus, to reveal ourselves, though tainted and distorted by sin, is holy. However, holy desires have sacred places; in marriage man and woman can sexually desire one another and be naked and unashamed, but only in marriage. Nakedness in marriage should be a testament to Christ's union with us and our union with our husbands. Our clothing outside of marriage should be a testament to that union as well.

WHAT NOW?

At this point, in many works on modesty, the author gives a list of "do's and don'ts" to consider when assessing clothing. The theological foundations seem "boring" and are hard to find in only too many Christian books, seminars, and conferences. It's easier to jump directly to the "rules." I have heard many young women sigh and turn away from these kinds of lists, seeing them as the "same old thing" delivered by those who are, they feel, out of touch. If, after understanding that modesty comes from holiness, you cannot decide for yourself what to put on, one of two possibilities is the truth: either you still don't understand the point, or you reject the point. The first is a misunderstanding; the second is sin.

To be fair, the world is confusing in its messages, and we as Christians are not invulnerable to the pressures of the bold, omnipresent allure of cultural patterns, fashion, self-confidence, and self-esteem. We hear so often that "if you've got it, flaunt it." Even the idea of blending in with culture—being relevant—is so prevalent and mainstream that choosing a sweater or skirt becomes a Herculean task. You're torn between wanting to be normal and wanting to do the right thing biblically and theologically. Sometimes, and I have heard this often too, you don't want to be a "prude." But thinking theologically is what Christ-in-us means. Everything we do matters. Everything we put on matters. The world tells us to throw off our clothing and to not be ashamed of our nakedness, to revel in womanhood and its potential power. And perhaps, by comparison to most of the women you see, you feel you're doing well.

But we don't need this power the world *seduces us* with. We don't need any other power but what is found in Jesus Christ. We are now in Christ, and we put Him on. We are not clothed with the "treasures" that this world affords. The confidence in Christ that we have does not give us license to showcase pieces of ourselves that were made for intimacy and union in sacred places. So to the world, confess who you are in Christ by showing who you are without Him—naked and ashamed.

DISCUSSION QUESTIONS

1. Why should we be ashamed of our nakedness?

2. Why is it important that God designed us to crave nakedness? How have we distorted that desire, and how does it show itself in the world today and in our own lives?

3. If your "intentions are good," or "you don't mean to draw attention to yourself," does it still matter what you wear?

4. In light of the theological arguments presented here, what changes might you make in the way you dress or present yourself to the world?

READING SUGGESTIONS

• FICTION: *Pride and Prejudice* by Jane Austen

• NONFICTION: *Girls Uncovered* by Joe S. McIlhaney Jr., MD, and Freda McKissic Bush, MD.; *A Return to Modesty: Discovering the Lost Virtue* by Wendy Shalit (read in the context of the chapter). As a point of interest, two women college students have written personal responses to Shalit's book charting their thinking about modesty and contemporary sexual attitudes. These can be found in the appendixes to *Unseduced and Unshaken*.

CHAPTER 10

IS IT WORTH IT? IS HE WORTHY?

BY ROSALIE DE ROSSET

WORTH: 1. The quality of something that renders it desirable, useful, or valuable.[1]

> But only one thing is needed. Mary has chosen what is better,
> and it will not be taken away from her.
>
> LUKE 10:42 (NIV)

W hen I was a young woman, I was always looking for a hero or heroine, someone to look up to, someone who went against the status quo, someone who spoke the truth in a way that inspired me. More often than not the person was a speaker or a teacher, almost always male, as that is who predominantly filled the podiums and platforms in my early life. I didn't want to get to know these people; I wanted to listen to them from afar. I wrote down the things they said and was inspired to study, to read Scripture, to pursue goodness and holiness. At this moment I could make a list of names going back to my early teens. Overall, this served me well, calling me to the integrity and dignity they displayed.

Among my first heroines was Helen Roseveare, missionary stateswoman and author of memorable missionary accounts. In the 1980s she came to speak in chapel at Moody Bible Institute. I was young, impressed as we all are at that time of life by appearance, though I had enough sense to know this was not what matters. Roseveare stood up in the pulpit, an "older woman" in a gray polyester suit. For twenty-five minutes, she described Christ's presence in her life in the midst of suffering, some of it unspeakable. After every story of loss, she asked herself, "Is it worth it?" then "Is He worthy?" A few particulars of her story are as follows. A brilliant graduate of Cambridge medical school, she went to the mission field in Zaire, reluctantly and perhaps begrudgingly. And troubles afflicted her;

she suffered the loss of most everything in those years while doing significant ministry. The worst pain came when she was captured during the country's civil war, beaten, imprisoned, and yes, raped— as a single woman who had committed her body to God and kept herself pure. During that awful night, she asked herself again, Is it worth it? Then, she had to ask, Is He worthy? Her conclusion was not a question. The audience sat in a sort of stunned silence at the end. She became a light of Christ to me that day—beautiful, almost angelic. I have never forgotten the experience; I still have students listen to that talk.

THE NATURE OF A HEROINE

I began a significant journey of growth after hearing Dr. Roseveare. First of all, my view of what it means to be a Christian heroine changed. In the years that followed that chapel, I read everything I could find by and about Helen Roseveare. What became clear to me, from her own stories, was that she was a flawed person who had let God use her. When I got over the sense of disappointment and surprise, I respected her honesty and realized the problem was my idealization, my need for those I admired to be bigger than life, as unlike me as possible.

It does not take a great deal of exposure to Christian biography and autobiography to know that every one of the central figures had flaws in his or her heart and mind, imperfections of personality and approach. Some of them were cold, some of them proud and dismissive; others had, in the vernacular, "control issues" or made major missteps along the way. Still others were easily discouraged or depressed. Some of them even neglected their families and were workaholics. Everyone carries some kind of injury that affects her life and must be tempered. This is the emotional legacy over which we have no choice. That was part of the story of *Jane Eyre* where I started; her sense of injustice had to be refined; she had to fill the void opened by her brutal childhood first with God.

Today's well-known names are no different. I had missed the point. When I got it, I was relieved and even more inspired. I knew God could use me too, regardless of my emotional inheritance, my battle scars, my unfinished-but-in-progress sanctification, which, when all is said and done, is God's business. And of course, as Ann Spangler writes in the introduction to a series of portraits of outstanding Christian women, "There is another legacy that does come to us by choice, the Christian legacy, the inheritance that becomes ours when we give our lives to Christ and are called by his name. Even so, it is a legacy which comes to us now only in part. It is a promise not fully realized until the life to come. Meanwhile, as St. Paul says, we 'press on toward the goal for the prize of the upward call of God in Christ Jesus.'"[2]

CHOOSING THE BETTER THING

In "pressing on," we can consciously choose this legacy, this new inheritance, a process that must be lived out in specific ways. Being a Christian is a specific business; vagueness is deadly. Giving you a start on the particulars has been what this book is about, an attempt to show you the better thing that Jesus commends His friend Mary for choosing in Luke 10:42. Our world is full of look-alikes, and only close attention to detail will bring discernment.

Many years ago when the actress Audrey Hepburn was alive, an Audrey Hepburn look-alike contest was held which actually included a photograph of the actress herself. She finished fourth in the contest, proof that imitators can fool just about anyone unless the onlooker is attentive. Attentiveness is what a skilled carpenter has when he knows that the detail in a new house has been compromised though the cosmetic appearance is in tact. He can touch a wall, look at a floor or ceiling and know the truth. It's what my sister, an expert seamstress, has when she looks at even expensive clothing and sees crooked seams and mismatched plaids.

Attentiveness is not in vogue today—the broad sweep of generalized impression or feeling is.

On my first trip to Europe, Audrey Hepburn was on my plane between Geneva, Switzerland and Rome, Italy. Filing out from my cabin through first class, I saw the thin shoulders, the aquiline chin, the gorgeous eyes. I was sure it must be she, and it was. When I read about the contest, I asked myself, if she had been placed in a line-up of look-alikes, how would I have known her? By attention to the smallest detail. By a certain tilt of the eyes I had seen in one of her movies, a way she had of moving her hands, a distinctive wistful smile on her lips, the look out of her eyes. Even though I had actually seen her, the only way I would have identified her in a group of look-alikes was by being attentive.

Attentiveness is not in vogue today—the broad sweep of generalized impression or feeling is. For lack of attentiveness, we make choices that are dangerous, that end up contradicting the spiritual center of our lives. Lack of attention does not make for good carpentry, sewing, or a faith that's worth it.

Which brings me to the second lesson I learned long ago from

Helen Roseveare, a theological lesson. The lesson of deciding what is worth it. Will it be hard to choose dignity over the ease of cultural adaptation; will it take discipline to ruthlessly look at all your attitudes and motivations, to live an undivided life, to free yourself from the array of distractions and cages waiting to entrap you at your doorstep? Will there be losses along the way? Will you be tempted to take the ghostly path. Yes. Is it worth it, you will ask yourself, perhaps often. On the heels of that question, ask yourself another—Is He worthy? Perhaps, you will need to know more about Him to be able to answer, which brings us back to the importance of theology, the importance of sitting at Christ's feet in conversation. Answering that question is at the core of every life, one I answer every year with greater passion. Yes. Oh yes.

In one memorable scene, Constantine sits next to Skeeter at the kitchen table and speaks wisdom and comfort into her life from her own background of being put down, kept in her place, and undervalued.

YOU CAN'T DO IT ALONE

In the contemporary, very popular novel *The Help* (a multilayered title), and in the subsequent movie, women, black and white, find their voices, but not without community, not without "help." Constantine, a beloved black maid, has been a significant nurturing influence on the narrator of the book. The daughter of a wealthy white Southern family and a girl who can't quite live the conventional way her mother would like her to, Skeeter needs a friend and guide. In one memorable scene, Constantine sits next to Skeeter at the kitchen table and speaks wisdom and comfort into her life from her own background of being put down, kept in her place, and undervalued. She teaches Skeeter to know her own mind. As Skeeter tells the story, "She pressed her thumb hard in the palm of my hand, something we both knew meant *Listen. Listen to me.*"

We have to resist the temptation to spend time only with those we are most like.

"Ever morning, until you dead in the ground, you gone have to make this decision." Constantine was so close, I could see the blackness of her gums. "You gone have to ask yourself, *Am I gone believe what them fools say about me today?*"

She kept her thumb pressed hard in my hand. I nodded that I understood. . . . All my life I'd been told what to believe about politics, coloreds, being a girl. But with Constantine's thumb pressed in my hand, I realized I actually had a choice in what I could believe.[3]

We cannot become dignified Christians who make good choices alone. At every stage of our lives we need a community of friends, alone and in groups, who will speak into our lives in different ways, to different degrees. We need those who will deliver us, as Carolyn Heilbrun puts it, from "the delusion of a passive life," a life of "too much closure," in which we say, "If he notices me, if I marry him, if I get into college, . . . if I get that job—there always seems to loom the possibility of something being over, settled, sweeping clear the way for contentment."[4] Among those friends must be honest, insightful individuals with grounded theological and intellectual interests (as described earlier) who push us a bit, who are not afraid to tell us the truth while still loving us, and who can also receive the same from us. C. S. Lewis has described well how that works: "As the friend proves worthy, mutual respect and admiration grow, and together, friends "fight . . . reach . . . argue [and] . . . pray" with each other.[5] We have to resist the temptation to spend time only with those we are most like. We are better for having friends who are varied in interests, lifestyles, and temperaments.

"Everyone talks about 'authentic community' but the specific benefits of friendship are not included in the discussion."

Friendship, however, as stated earlier, and as Lewis and others have pointed out, does not get the attention, encouragement, or validation that every other form of relational love, including erotic or romantic love and love of family gets, even though it is, in its true form, the least selfish of all human connections. After all, one does not choose family, and passion is the impetus for romantic relationships. In contrast, healthy friendship begins by choice, without emotional volatility, based on mutual interests, ideas, and experiences.

Yet, ironically and sadly, if anything, friendship is undervalued and even suspected at times. The broader American culture and the evangelical subculture have almost made a god of marriage and family; young people are pressured early to "get going" in this direction.

One of my students said, "We're told generally that it's important to have friends, but no one talks about the value of *lasting* friendships." She added, "Everyone talks about 'authentic community' but the specific benefits of friendship are not included in the discussion." In fact, as another young woman noted, "friendship is not even addressed; everything else seems to be more important." It is no wonder then that one often sees women diminishing, neglecting, and even dropping their friendships with other women for the sake of their dating lives, putting a pressure and expectation on the dating process it cannot sustain or may even be crippled by. How often I have heard girls tell me that they seldom see a good friend anymore because "she's dating." And too often, women accept that loss because it has come to seem appropriate, even expected. Friendship is sacrificed to the culturally prioritized romantic relationship, not appreciated for the inestimable contribution it makes to a fully realized life.

Affirming the problem, Eugene Peterson writes that "friendship is a much underestimated aspect of spirituality. It's every bit as significant as prayer and fasting. Like the sacramental use of water and bread and wine, friendship takes what's common in human experience and turns it into something holy." Peterson then refers to the much-addressed friendship between David and Jonathan and says that it was "essential to David's life." In fact, he adds, "It's highly unlikely that David could have persisted in serving Saul without the friendship of Jonathan. . . . Jonathan's friendship entered David's soul in a way that Saul's hatred never did."[6]

Friends have been true mirrors to me, showing me myself, reflecting back to me an ugly spot in my soul, and reminding me of something good I had thought or done when I couldn't remember.

Friends have told me the truth about a direction I was headed or a relationship I had chosen. They have brought me back from the brink of disaster. Friends have prayed for me faithfully when I was sick, when I was overwhelmed by too great a task. Friends have written notes at just the right time, made a phone call, or come for a visit. With friends I have had the great conversations of my life. Those friends have been younger, older, and my age; few of them have had the same education or occupation as I have. More than anything, my best friends have always been mutual, receiving and giving, listening and talking, and above all remembering—remembering what is important to me and asking the right questions. I am fortunate to have a number of friendships still present in my life that go back decades, some of them to my childhood, a number to my young adulthood. They call to mind my history, the geography of my life's events, and more important, they preserve the map of my mind and spirit.

He speaks with righteous anger, He rebukes, He cries over the stubborn and the lost; He is filled with sadness over His own forsakenness.

We also need Constantines, the imput of older women who can guide us through the sometimes dense foliage of conflicting messages and complicated choices, who press their thumbs hard into our hands and remind us not to believe foolishness about being a girl. Sometimes there have been too few of these who are prepared to tell the truth which means that no matter where you find yourself in life, *you* need to be a Constantine yourself to someone younger.

THE FOUNDATION

Of course, the foundation of our community must be the Word of God. Few people have described what that looks like better than Dietrich Bonhoeffer in his little book *Life Together*. He urges us with great passion to "know the Scriptures. . . ." because "it is not our heart that determines our course, but God's Word." The Word, he continues is the corrective to people's constantly using their life experiences as the impetus for crucial decisions. "How shall we ever help a Christian brother [or sister] and set him straight in his difficulty and doubt, if not with God's own Word? . . . The existence of any Christian life together depends on whether . . . it distinguish[es] between a human ideal and God's reality, between spiritual and human community."[7]

And oh, what you will find. God, working through the hands of the biblical authors, was a good writer, particularly apt at characterization, one of the most important qualities of literary writing. I want to encourage each woman reading this to pay attention to the Gospels. Christ's emotional complexity and expressions are riveting when looked at closely. He is not a pallid figure, white robed, blue towel over the arm, brown-eyed, serene, and quiet as we too often see Him, the kind of guy as one of my students put it, "who would never look at me." He speaks with righteous anger, He rebukes, He cries over the stubborn and the lost; He is filled with sadness over His own forsakenness. He defends children and women with authority. And He loves, taking every individual seriously, an act that infuses that individual with the beginnings of dignity.

In one of her strange and thought-provoking stories called "A Temple of the Holy Ghost" (an allusion to 1 Corinthians 6:19), American author Flannery O'Connor paints a striking scene which goes to the heart of how much Christ values us and seeks to dignify us. In it, two fourteen-year-old girls who are going to school at a convent have come to stay with their aunt and a very alert twelve-year-old cousin while they are on break. The girls are silly, "not very bright," and interested only in boys, and they call themselves "Temple One" and "Temple Two" while they "shake with laughter." When their aunt asks them why they do this, they explain that Sister Perpetua at the convent has admonished them that should a young man behave "in an ungentlemanly manner with them in the back of an automobile," they are to say "Stop sir! I am a Temple of the Holy Ghost!" This, the nun has told them, will halt such behavior. While the fourteen-year-olds consider this an enormous joke, the twelve-year-old is deeply struck by the admonition, and she repeats to herself, "I am a Temple of the Holy Ghost" and is "pleased with the phrase. It made her feel like someone had given her a present."[8]

That young girl is precisely right—she knows in her young spirit that being a temple of the Holy Ghost is not a restriction; it is a lovely, loving present. Christ so loves us that He wants our entire selves (body, soul, and spirit) to be His dwelling place, setting us free *not* to sin, setting us free *from* the enslavement of cultural pressures and the lies we are told and which we tell ourselves. Freed, we can as Luther once said, dance with God, expressing our longings in ways that will not injure us, and living whole, undivided lives, as, yes, His temple.

"Be Thou my dignity, Thou my delight" reads a line from an ancient Irish hymn. The connection couldn't be more powerfully expressed. With Christ as our dignity, our desire is met.

IT SHOULDN'T BE EASY

BY RACHEL SCHLAGEL

My whole life I have been instructed by my Christian leaders, pastors, parents, friends, etc., to be modest. I have been told that modesty comes from within. I have been told that to dress modestly is to respect my Christian brothers so as to prevent them from falling into lust. I have also been told that modesty is a way of showing self-respect and prevents others from thinking I am easy and have low self-esteem.

A book assigned in a class revolutionized my thinking. What most intrigued me about *A Return to Modesty* is the fact that Wendy Shalit, its author, is not a Christian. From the first chapter, Shalit gives the background of her life and conservative, Jewish upbringing. She explains the values her parents placed in her and also proudly describes her grandparents' wonderful marriage. Why is it that when she looks at pictures of an engaged Jewish couple touching each other, she can see a glow and happiness that she does not see in her peers? Maybe it's because marriage has so much more to offer than casual dating and sex. Maybe it's because modesty, mystery, and innocence lead to real love.

Shalit's book is countercultural. She writes about her public school experience and her parents' decision to take her out of sex education. Although she had no idea what she was missing out on, she quickly realized that because she missed out on being educated, she was not suffering the brunt of many eight-year-old boys' sexual jokes. This made me think of my public school experience. When I was in fourth grade, all the girls were invited after school to watch a video with their moms that taught us about puberty, menstruation, deodorant, and emotions. Although I still did not know what sex explicitly was, I felt my childhood coming to an end as my girlfriends and I whispered to one another at lunchtime about whether or not we had yet started our "P," as we called it. By sixth grade, we went on a field trip, not any ordinary field trip where you get to go to a zoo or a skating rink. This field trip was a sex education field trip. I will never forget my horror when I found out what happened during sex.

Shalit stresses the need to protect innocence. Fortunately, my parents did not allow me to watch MTV or R-rated movies until I was seventeen. Unfortunately, I went to public school and quickly learned a lot through it. I remember pretending I knew what people were talking about so as to not reveal my innocence and thus be embarrassed. Shalit points out how pop culture magazine covers encourage women to live life to the fullest, have sex, have fun, and yet on the same cover, give women tips on how to snag the "right" guy. It is incredibly contradictory. Culture tells us to have sex, live for our desires, and be free. Our hearts tell us to wait and yearn to be loved, admired, and pursued. Shalit explains the phenomenon that women become emotionally attached to their sex partners. Women were not made to take sex casually. Casual sex leads to disappointment, shame, fear, and regret.

This book has reminded me that it is okay to want a romantic relationship. It has reminded me that I want to be pursued. I want a man to see that I am worth more than just the way I look and how much he can get from me. Unfortunately, because of believing what my culture tells me, I have believed that I need to be open to a lack of respect and honor on a man's part in order for him to like me. I have given up on wanting a man to pursue me, because I don't think there are men out there who are wanting to be honorable and respectful.

My deepest desire in my next relationship, whether it be someone I casually date or a serious relationship, is to not have a hint of sexual immorality. I want to show the world that I conduct myself differently. I want a relationship that is romantic, full of mystery and self-control. I want to ultimately know that the man loves me for who I am, and not just for what I can give him. Realizing that I have this desire should encourage me to dress and act in a way that is modest in all areas of my life. I need to be discreet in what I tell boys that I date, and I need to be respectful in the way I dress. I do not need to prove to any boy "what I got" through the way I dress and how I act with him.

While I was reading this book, a boy asked me on a date through a text message. At first I was quick to reply "Sure." But when he texted back and asked me when we could go out, it hit me how inappropriate it was that he asked me in a text message. *A text message.* After a few hours of thought (that's a long time in my fast-paced culture), I responded that I was flattered that he would want to take me out, but I was disappointed that he hadn't asked me in person.

It used to be that asking someone out over the phone was inappropriate. Now, that is not only viewed as chivalrous, but texting a message is also acceptable. Text messaging has allowed people to be accessible instantly as well as secretively, with no risk. It is now expected that everyone is accessible all the time, so the thought of having to wait a few days or even a few weeks to bump into the person one wants to ask is inconceivable. I say this boy should wait to find me in person, and during that time he is waiting to cross paths with me to ask me on a date, he pray about it! My culture is fast-paced and impulsive; self-control and discipline hardly exist anymore. If I hadn't just read this book, I probably would have said yes and met the boy that next afternoon to "get to know each other." I don't want it to be that easy, and now I have the encouragement to keep believing and thinking that it doesn't have to be.

"SO MUCH FROM SO LITTLE"

BY CARA COLEMAN

I n the introduction of *A Return to Modesty* by Wendy Shalit, I was intrigued by the beaming, love-struck Jewish couple who had never even touched one another. I thought that that sounded a bit extreme and unrealistic, but still beautiful. This book has profoundly impressed upon me that one of the most precious gifts in life is innocence. Innocence once taken can never be regained.

The culture we live in now barely gives us a chance to be innocent. We live in a society where sex education is taught in kindergarten, where pornography is everywhere in and outside the home, and where children are sexually abused. Innocence is stolen. The first half of Shalit's book was overwhelming in its shocking descriptions of a sexualized culture where multiple sexual partners and hook-ups are the norm leading to a culture where rape, street harassment, eating disorders, and pornography addictions are also the norm. Women are told to be like men, that there is no difference between men and women, that they can and should have sex often with no attachments, and that to dream or believe in romance means that you are delusional. We are taught that to be good at sex or to be wanted by men means that we need to have experience. Women think that we are being revolutionary by setting ourselves free sexually. But really we are just being like everyone else and following the normative patterns laid before us by our culture. What would really be revolutionary, says Shalit, would be to return to modesty.

Shalit defines modesty as follows:

> . . . A reflex, arising naturally to help women protect her hopes and guide their fulfillment—specifically, this hope for one man. . . . Most women would prefer one man stick by them, for better or for worse, to a series of men who abandon them. Of course, along with this hope comes a certain vulnerability, because every time a man fails to stick by us, our hopes are, in a sense, dashed. This is where modesty fits in. For modesty armed this special vulnerability—not to oppress women, but with the aim of putting them on equal footing with men. The delay modesty created not only made it more likely that women could select men that would stick by them, but in turning lust into love, it changed men from uncivilized males who ran after as many sexual partners as they could get to men who really wanted to stick by one woman.[1]

Shalit also talks about men's role in modesty and about modesty being natural. Just watch girls on a windy day holding on to their skirts. Modesty is built into us. Most women, when asked why they wear tight or low-cut clothing even if they don't like it, answer that it is the style or that it is expected of them. Young girls are shy around boys naturally, and each culture in the world has some part of their body that women would rather die than expose. Being modest is far more natural than exposing everything. In relation to men, women have helped make men what they are now.

By not respecting ourselves and by showing everything and giving everything for free and without commitment on the part of a man, we have made and continued the cycle of men using women as prostitutes without having to pay, men who don't commit, and men who think that girls who get attached are the problem. If all women carried themselves with dignity and demanded respect, and women started changing the way they view modesty, men would have no choice but to change as well.

This issue with modesty is really about dignity. Women on the whole do not have the nobility of character or the self-respect to be modest in a culture that tells them that it is uncool or abnormal to do so. We are so worried about fitting in and being normal that we neglect how we actually feel about things and what the consequences of accepting the culture are.

In my favorite chapter of the book entitled "Modesty and the Erotic," Shalit argues that "the kind of allure that lasts is what modesty protects and inspires."[2] Being modest is not the same as being a prude. It was such a new idea to me that promiscuity and prudery both say that "nothing fazes me" but that modesty is a true sign that you "can be moved and it issues the invitation for one man to try."[3] Shalit tells a story about her loss of innocence that was mind-blowing to me. As she starts to tell the story of going to her camp counselor's room late at night, I am sure she is going to say that she slept with him or she was raped. Instead, she says he touched her hair, and that she got freaked out and left. She took a guilty shower that night, and all he did was touch her hair. Just from him touching her hair she felt "so much from so little."[4] It made so much sense to me that when something has been done over and over, it grows dull and loses its excitement and meaning. I had never thought about that in regard to sex. Something as little as having your hair touched can completely intoxicate you when you have been modest. Every touch is exhilarating for someone who has never been touched.

Shalit says that people long for others to care and for parents to interfere. We still have a sense that when we are kissing on the sidewalk, someone should come up to us and say that we are disturbing them. But, as a whole, we have become desensitized and nothing fazes us. It made me realize how others are raised in this culture. If I'm ever a parent, I will care. I will talk with my daughters about what they see and wear and how late they are out and with whom. I will talk to my sons about how to treat women, and I want my husband to be an example of that.

The world has had an effect on me. I have believed lies about myself, ones I fight daily directly from culture. I have believed that I have to be strong and independent as a woman and not rely on anyone else, especially men. I have believed that I am fat and ugly and that without a good deal of work and money I will always be that way. But sexually I have never been touched, seen images, or even been jeered at inappropriately. Why did the Lord choose to allow me to walk through my life untouched physically, unimpressed by images, and unscathed by words? I will never know the answers, but I am grateful.

The innocence that I have lived in for so long is only because of the Lord's direct protection in my life. I went to public school and never once was asked on a date or to a party, or pressured to drink, smoke, or do anything with boys. This is nothing short of miraculous. In our culture, one has to make a conscious decision to be modest, be dignified, and have restraint—values no longer taught by teachers and adults. If I ever have children, I pray that the Lord would graciously protect their innocence as He has graciously protected mine, and that they would choose to be set apart and believe that they are worth more than what they are told.

NOTES

INTRODUCTION

1. C. S. Lewis, "Introduction," *St. Athanasius on the Incarnation*, translated and edited by A Religious of C.S.M.V. (London: A.R. Mowbray & Co. Limited, 1963), 4.

CHAPTER 1: MINDING YOUR DIGNITY

1. This definition represents a compilation from *Merriam Webster Dictionary* and *The American Heritage Dictionary*, 2nd College ed., s.v. "dignity."

2. J. R. Jones, "Jane Eyre's Mystery Man," *The Reader* (March 17, 2011): 21.

3. Os Guinness, Virginia Mooney, and Karen Lee-Thorp, *When No One Sees: the Importance of Character in an Age of Image* (Colorado Springs, Colo: Navpress, 2000), 15.

4. A. O. Scott, "Radiant Spirit Blossoms in Barren Land," *New York Times* (March 10, 2011).

5. *The American Heritage Dictionary*, 2nd College ed., s.v. "spirited."

6. Lana Norris, untitled, (e-mail, November 8, 2011).

7. *The American Heritage Dictionary*, 2nd College ed., s.v. "poise."

8. Ronald H. Rottschafer, "The Passive Christian," *Reformed Journal* 33, no. 12, (December 1, 1983): 11–12.

9. Charlotte Brontë and Michael Mason, *Jane Eyre* (London: Penguin Books, 1996), 41.

10. Ibid., 125–26.

11. Ibid., 281.

12. Ibid., Preface, 6.

13. Ibid., 356.

14. *The American Heritage Dictionary*, 2nd College ed., s.v. "indomitable."

15. Brontë, *Jane Eyre*, 356.

16. I am indebted for this phrasing to Ken Gire, *Windows of the Soul: Experiencing God in New Ways* (Grand Rapids, Mich: Zondervan Pub. House, 1996), 48.

17. Ibid.

CHAPTER 2: FINDING YOUR VOICE

1. Dana Crowley Jack, "Silencing the self: Inner dialogues and outer realities," in Thomas E. Joiner and James C. Coyne, eds., *The Interactional Nature of Depression: Advances in Interpersonal Approaches* (Washington, D.C.: American Psychological Association, 1999), 221–46.

2. *The American Heritage Dictionary,* 2nd College ed., s.v., "voice."

3. Charlotte Brontë and Michael Mason, *Jane Eyre* (London: Penguin Books, 1996),

4. Dana Crowley Jack, "Silencing the self," 225.

5. Mayo Foundation for Medical Education and Research, "Depression in Women: Understanding the Gender Gap: About Twice as Many Women as Men Experience Depression. Several Factors May Increase a Woman's Risk of Depression," http://www.mayoclinic.com/health/depress/MH00035.

6. Dana Crowley Jack, "Silencing the self," 225.

7. Gen. 16:8

8. Gen. 16:13 (NIV)

9. 1 Sam. 25:17

10. 1 Sam. 25:3 (NIV)

11. 1 Sam. 25:17 (NIV)

12. 1 Sam. 25:18 (NIV)

13. 1 Sam. 25:29 (NIV)

14. Dana Crowley Jack, "Silencing the self," 226.

15. Dorothy Sayers, *Are Women Human?* (Grand Rapids: Eerdmans, 1992), 47.

CHAPTER 3: LONGING: FROM DISPARITY TO DESIRE

1. Merriam Webster Dictionary, 11th ed., s.v. "desire," and "disparate."

2. 1 Cor. 13:12

3. Cassandra Golds, *The Museum of Mary Child* (Tulsa, Oklahoma: Kane Miller, 2009), 133.

4. Ibid.

5. Ibid.

6. Ibid., 132.

7. Jane Austen, *Pride and Prejudice* (New York: Greenwich House, Crown Publishers, Inc., 1982), 221.

8. Ibid., 223.

9. Ibid., 232.

10. Ibid., 236–37.

11. Aleksandr Solzhenitsyn, *The Gulag Archipelago, 1918–1956; An Experiment in Literary Investigation* (New York: Harper & Row, 1974–78). I was reminded of this quote while reading Brent Curtis, "Less-Wild Lovers Standing at the Crossroads of Desire," *Mars Hill Review*, 8 (Summer, 1997), 13.

12. Rom. 21b–23 (NIV)

13. Plato, W. C. Helmbold, and Wilson Gerson Rabinowitz, *Phaedrus* (Indianapolis: Bobbs-Merrill Educational Pub., 1984), x.

14. H. M. Daleski, *The Divided Heroine, A Recurrent Pattern in Six English Novels* (New York: Holmes & Meier Publishers, 1984), 3.

15. Ibid., 3.

16. Ibid.

17. Ibid.

18. Merriam Webster Dictionary, 11th ed., s.v. "discretion."

19. Larry Crabb, *Inside Out* (Colorado Springs: NavPress, 1988), 212.

20. Ibid., 14.

21. Ibid., 83.

22. Ibid.

23. The cartoon was first published in the *Chicago Tribune*, Chicago, IL.

24. C. S. Lewis, *Surprised by Joy: The Shape of My Early Life* (New York: Harvest, 1955), 18.

25. Ibid.

26. C. S. Lewis, *The Pilgrim's Regress: An Allegorical Apology for Christianity* (Grand Rapids: Eerdmans, Pub. Co., 1977), 8.

27. Sherwood Anderson, "Adventure," in *Winesburg, Ohio* (New York: Penguin, 1993), 103–12.

28. Brent Curtis, "Less-Wild Lovers: Standing at the Crossroads of Desire," *Mars Hill Review*, 8 (Summer, 1997), 9–10.

29. Ibid., 10.

30. Ibid., 17.

31. Francis Thompson, *The Hound of Heaven* (Wilton, Connecticut: Morehouse-Barlow, 1988).

CHAPTER 4: "EVERYTHING IS THEOLOGICAL"

1. Marvin R. Wilson, *Our Father Abraham: Jewish Roots of the Christian Faith* (Grand Rapids: W. B. Eerdmans, 1989), 156.

2. *American Heritage Dictionary*, 2nd College ed., s.v. "theology."

3. Dorothy Sayers, *Creed or Chaos?* (Manchester, NH: Sophia Institute Press, 1995), 19.

4. Mortimer Adler as quoted by James Sire in *Habits of the Mind: Intellectual Life as a Christian Calling* (Downers Grove: Intervarsity Press, 2000), 27.

5. Shirley Chisholm, "I'd Rather Be Black Than Female," *McCalls*, 97, no. 6, (August, 1970), 6, as cited in "Seeing the Invisible Prejudice" by Rosalie de Rosset in *Building Unity in the Church*, ed. Dwight Perry (Chicago: Moody Press, 2002), 221.

6. Ibid,, 221–22.

7. Mrs. Ellen J. Foster, "Work for Women," *The Institute Tie*, 9, no. 6, (Feb. 1909), 483.

8. Dorothy Sayers, *Are Women Human?* (Grand Rapids: W. B. Eerdmans, 1992), 12–13, 19.

9. Mrs. Ellen J. Foster, "Work for Women," 483.

10. Dorothy L. Sayers, "Dorothy L. Sayers to Muriel Jaeger, January 11, 1919, Wade document 22/108," in *Creed Without Chaos: Exploring Theology in the Writings of Dorothy Sayers*, Laura K. Simmons (Grand Rapids: Baker Academic, 2005), 67.

11. Gustave Oehler, *The International Standard Bible Encylcopedia*, vol. 5, ed. J. Orr, (Grand Rapids: Eerdmans, 1952), 2838. I am indebted for this reference to Alice Mathews, *Preaching That Speaks to Women* (Grand Rapids: Baker Academic, 2003), 47.

12. Remarks quoted here are from students in a homiletics class taught in the spring of 2011 at Moody Bible Institute.

13. Alice Mathews, *Preaching That Speaks to Women*, 90.

14. Dorothy Sayers, *Creed or Chaos?*, 24.

15. Carolyn Custis James, *When Life and Beliefs Collide: How Knowing God Makes a Difference* (Grand Rapids: Zondervan, 2001), 20.

16. Dorothy Sayers, *Creed or Chaos?*, 24–25.

17. Alice Mathews, *Preaching That Speaks to Women*, 90.

18. Carolyn Custis James, *When Life and Beliefs Collide*, 19.

19. Ibid.

20. Dorothy Sayers, *Creed or Chaos?*, 47.

21. Alice Mathews, *A Woman God Can Use* (Grand Rapids: Discovery House, 1990), 3.

22. Ibid., 9.

23. J. I. Packer, *Knowing God* (Downers Grove: InterVarsity Press, 1973), 14–15. I was reminded of this reference by its citation in Carolyn Custis-James, *When Life and Beliefs Collide*.

24. Amy Carmichael, "The Last Defile," *The Treasury of Christian Poetry*, edited by Lorraine Eitel, et al. (Old Tappan, N.J.: Fleming H. Revell Co., 1982), 85.

CHAPTER 5: DISTRACTED OR DIGNIFIED?

1. *The American Heritage Dictionary*, 2nd College ed., s.v. "distracted," and "genuine."

2. Charlotte Brontë and Michael Mason, *Jane Eyre* (London: Penguin Books, 1996), 215.

3. George Eliot and Gordon Sherman Haight, *Middlemarch* (Boston: Houghton Mifflin Co, 1956), 6.

4. C. S. Lewis, *The Great Divorce* (New York: Collier Books, 1946), 76.

5. *The American Heritage Dictionary*, 2nd College ed., s.v., "ghost."

6. Agnieszka Zelinska, "Heed the Discord," *Moody Student* (April 13, 1999): 7.

7. Jean Kilbourne, *Deadly Persuasion: Why Women and Girls Must Fight the Addictive Power of Advertising* (New York: The Free Press, 1999), 132–33.

8. Ibid., 133.

9. Susan Shapiro Barash, *Tripping the Prom Queen: The Truth About Women and Rivalry* (New York: St. Martin's Press, 2006), 89.

10. Louise Bernikow, "Cinderella: Saturday Afternoon at the Movies," *Perspectives on Contemporary Issues: Readings across the Disciplines*, 2nd ed., ed. Katherine Anne Ackley (Fort Worth, TX: Harcourt, 2000), 360–67.

11. Lisa See, *Snow Flower and the Secret Fan: A Novel* (New York: Random House, 2005).

12. Doug Peterson, "Is Christianity Only Meant For Pretty Women?" *The Wittenberg Door*, 124 (July/Aug. 1992): 26.

13. Ibid.

14. Ibid.

15. Bethany Pierce, *Feeling for Bones* (Chicago: Moody Publishers, 2007), 281–82.

16. Mary Ellen Ashcroft, *Temptations Women Face* (Downers Grove: InterVarsity Press, 1991), 31, 38

17. Amy Koehler, librarian, Moody Bible Institute, November 28, 2011.

18. Julianna Gustafson, "Protesting Victoria," *The Horizon*, Westmont College Student Newspaper, February 1996.

19. Mary Ellen Ashcroft, *Temptations Women Face*, 77.

20. Malcom Muggeridge, *Jesus Rediscovered* (Wheaton: Tyndale Publishers, 1971), 64.

21. Mary Ellen Ashcroft, *Temptations Women Face*, 86–87.

22. Kate Chopin, *The Awakening* in *The American Tradition in Literature*, 11th ed. vol II, ed. George Perkins and Barbara Perkins (New York: McGraw Hill, 2007), 646.

23. I'm indebted to Jane Dwyer, *Jane Austen* (New York: Continuum, 1989), 53–63 for seeing Austen's perspective.

24. Ibid.

25. For danger signals that are even darker see various editions of Focus Newsletter, http://members.aol.com/focusnews1. Located in Elmhurst, Illinois, Focus Ministries, headed by Paula Silva, is devoted to helping women who find themselves emotionally or physically abused and to educating young women in how to make good dating choices. The website provides pertinent information. Also helpful is Sandra Scott's book called *Charmers and Con Artists & Their Flip Side* (Winepress Pub., 2000).

26. Mary Whelchel, *Common Mistakes Singles Make* (Old Tappan, New Jersey: Revell Pub. Co., 1985), 43–66.

CHAPTER 6: MINDFUL OR MINDLESS

1. *The American Heritage Dictionary*, 2nd College ed., s.v. "classic."

2. Ibid., "leisure."

3. Charlotte Brontë and Michael Mason, *Jane Eyre* (London: Penguin Books, 1996), 215.

4. Charles Krauthammer, "Holocaust: Memory and resolve," *Time*, 141, no. 18, (May 3, 1993): 84.

5. Marva J. Dawn, *Reaching Out Without Dumbing Down: A Theology of Worship for the Turn-of-the-Century Culture* (Grand Rapids, Mich: W. B. Eerdmans, 1995), 58–59.

6. Marvin R. Wilson, *Our Father Abraham: Jewish Roots of the Christian Faith*, (Grand Rapids, Mich: W. B. Eerdmans, 1999), 156.

7. *The American Heritage Dictionary*, 2nd College ed., s.v. "leisure."

8. Various, unpublished student Media Fast papers, college writing class, Moody Bible Institute (Fall, 2010).

9. One of the most important books any thinking Christian should read on technology is Neil Postman's *Amusing Ourselves to Death: Public Discourse in the Age of Show Business* (New York: Penguin Books, 1986), a penetrating analysis of television, whose principles are widely applicable.

10. Richard Winter, *Still Bored in a Culture of Entertainment: Rediscovering Passion and Wonder* (Downers Grove, Ill: InterVarsity Press, 2002), 35–36.

11. Josef Pieper, *Leisure: The Basis of Culture* (Indianapolis: Liberty Fund, 1999), 30–31.

12. John Piper, *A Hunger for God: Desiring God Through Fasting and Prayer* (Wheaton, Ill: Crossway Books, 1997), 14.

13. Marva J. Dawn, *Reaching Out*, 188.

CHAPTER 7: READING AS A SPIRITUAL EXERCISE

1. *The American Heritage Dictionary*, 2nd College ed., s.v. "romance," "imagination."

2. Louise Cowan, "The Importance of the Classics," in *Invitation to the Classics*, eds., Louise Cowan and Os Guinness (Grand Rapids: Baker Books, 1998), 21.

3. Gene Edward Vieth Jr., *Reading Between the Lines: a Christian Guide to Literature* (Wheaton: Crossway Books, 1990), xiv.

4. Michael, Flaherty, "Let Them At Least Have Heard of Brave Knights and Heroic Courage," *Imprimis*, 36, no. 2 (Feb. 2007).

5. Books which present an apologetics for fiction are the following:

   Cowan, Louise. "The Importance of the Classics," In *Invitation to the Classics*, eds., Louise Cowan and Os Guinness. Grand Rapids: Baker Books, 1998.
   Reinke, Tony. *Lit!: A Christian Guide to Reading Books.* Wheaton: Crossway Books, 2011.
   Ryken, Leland. *Windows to the World: Literature in Christian Perspective.* Grand Rapids: Zondervan, 1985.
   Veith, Gene Edward, Jr. *Reading Between the Lines: A Christian Guide to Literature.* Wheaton: Crossway Books, 1990.

6. C. S. Lewis, *The Voyage of the Dawn Treader* (New York: Collier Books, 1970), 1–2.

7. Ibid., 71.

8. Mike Yaconelli, "Reading Can Be Dangerous," *The Wittenberg Door*, 10, no. 5, (January 21, 1977), 26.

9. T. S. Eliot. Quoted by Earl F. Palmer in *Salvation by Surprise: Studies in the Book of Romans* (Waco, Tex: Word Books, 1975), 44.

10. Romance Writers of America, "About the Romance Genre: Romance Literature Statistics: Readership Statistics," http://www.rwa.org/cs/readership_state. The RWA's statistics result from two studies commissioned by the association. One study—on the sales of romance fiction—is compiled by RWA from Simba Information (an independent market research firm that studies the publishing industry), R. R. Bowker's Books In Print, the AAP, and other named sources. This study is updated every 12 months. Another study focuses on reader demographics, book content, and book-buying habits. The 2009 survey was conducted by InfoTrends, Inc. This first version of this study was conducted in 1998. The follow-up surveys were conducted in Summer/Fall 2002 and Winter 2005."

11. Romance Writers of America, "About the Romance Genre." http://www.rwa.org/cs/the_romance_genre.

12. Ann Barr Snitow, "Mass Market Romance: Pornography for Women is Different," in *The Pop Culture Zone: Writing Critically About Popular Culture*, eds. Allison Smith, Trixie G. Smith, and Stacia Watkins (Boston, MA: Wadsworth, Cengage, 2009), 534–35.

13. Ibid.

14. Ibid., 553.

15. Carol Falkenstein, "Bella's Paradise: Just a Bite Away" (unpublished review, August 2011).

16. Paul DeParrie, *Romanced to Death: The Sexual Seduction of American Culture* (Brentwood, Tenn: Wohgemuth & Hyatt, 1989).

17. Susan Verstraete, "Christian Romance Novels: Are They Our Harmless Little Secret?" http://bulletininserts.org/bulletininsert.aspx?bulletininsert_id+94.

18. Janice Radway, "Women Read the Romance: The Interaction of Text and Context," in *The Pop Culture Zone: Writing Critically about Popular Culture*, 548, 553.

19. Susan Verstraete, "Christian Romance Novels."

20. Crystal Rae Nelson, "A Warning Against Christian Romance Novels: The Dangers of Romanticism," Good Morals, http://www.goodmorals.org/crystal.htm.

21. Allan Bloom, *Love and Friendship* (New York: Schuster and Schuster, 1993), 210–11.

22. Gustave Flaubert and Paul De Man, *Madame Bovary: Backgrounds and sources; essays in criticism* (New York: W. W. Norton, 1965), 24, 41.

23. Ibid., 48.

24. Ibid., 77.

25. Ibid., 117.

26. Madeleine L'Engle, "Icons of the True," in *Shadow & Light: Literature and the Life of Faith*, eds. Darryl L. Tippens, Jeanne Murray Walker, and Stephen Weathers (Abilene, TX: ACU Press, 2005), 71.

27. Charlotte Gordon, *Mistress Bradstreet: The Untold Life of America's First Poet* (New York: Little, Brown and Co., 2005), cover flyleaf.

28. Ibid., 69.

CHAPTER 8: SEXUAL DIGNITY

1. *The American Heritage Dictionary*, 2nd College ed., s.v. "chastity."

2. Charlotte Brontë and Michael Mason, *Jane Eyre* (London: Penguin Books, 1996): 227.

3. C. S. Lewis, *Mere Christianity* (New York: Macmillan Pub. Co., 1976), 89.

4. Mark Regnerus, *Forbidden Fruit: Sex and Religion in the Lives of American Teenagers* (Oxford: Oxford University Press, 2009), 203–7.

5. Lauren Winner, *Real Sex* (Grand Rapids: Brazos Press, 2005), 14. This book is one of the best I have read on the subject. Winner gives an unclichéd, compassionate yet uncompromising biblical treatment of chastity—its foundation, its difficulties, its relationship community.

6. Ibid., 15.

7. Archibald Hart, *The Sexual Man* (Dallas: Word Pub., 1994), 204.

8. *Merriam Webster's Dictionary*, 11th ed., s.v., "even."

9. Erwin Lutzer, "Rescued from the Folly of Self-Salvation," sermon preached at The Moody Memorial Church, Chicago, IL, October 16, 2011.

10. Lisa Graham McMinn, *Growing Strong Daughters: Encouraging Girls to Become All They're Meant to Be*, revised edition (Grand Rapids: Baker Books, 2008), 133.

11. Archiubald Hart, 204.

12. Lisa Graham McMinn, 133.

13. Ibid., 138.

14. Journal entries used with permission from client.

15. Safe Families, "Statistics on Pornography, Sexual Addiction and Online Perpetrators," http://www.safefamilies.org/sfStats.php.

16. I am indebted to Tammy Perlmutter who made me aware of this organization besides providing other invaluable resources.

17. Journal entries used with permission from client.

18. Reinhard Hütter, "Pornography and Acedia," *First Things* 222 (April 2012): 47.

19. For a striking account of pornography's dangers and devastation of one family, read Laurie Hall, *An Affair of the Mind* (Wheaton, IL: Tyndale House Publishers, 2003).

20. Alice Miller, As cited by Mary Pipher, *Reviving Ophelia: Saving the Selves of Adolescent Girls* (New York: G. P. Putnam & Sons, 1999), 44.

21. Mark Regnerus, *Forbidden Fruit*, 116, 115.

22. Archibald Hart, 47.

23. Lewis B. Smedes, *Sex for Christians: The Limits and Liberties of Sexual Living* (Grand Rapids: Eerdmans Pub. Co., 1976), 245.

24. Walter Trobisch and Ingrid Hult Trobisch, *My Beautiful Feeling: Correspondence with Ilona* (Downers Grove, Ill: InterVarsity Press, 1976). While the book is out of print, it is available through online sources and also through libraries. http://www.worldcat.org/oclc/2694896.

25. Ibid., 7–9.

26. Ibid., 21.

27. Ibid., 11, 18.

28. Gale Berkowitz, "UCLA Study on Friendship Among Women: An Alternative to Fight or Flight. Dec. 18, 2009. http://www.anapsid.org/cnd/gender/tendfend.html.

29. See C. S. Lewis, "Of Friendship," in *The Four Loves* (New York: Harcourt, Brace Janovich, 1960).

30. Janelle Hallman, *The Heart of Female Same-Sex Attraction* (Downer's Grove: InterVarsity, 2008), 268.

31. Archibald Hart, *The Sexual Man*, 204.

32. C. S. Lewis, *The Weight of Glory* (New York: Macmillan Pub. Co., 1980), 5.

33. Lauren Winner, *Real Sex*, 137.

34. William Shakespeare, "The Expense of Spirit," in *Great Sonnets*, Edited by Paul Negri (New York: Dover Publications, 1994), 15.

35. Archibald Hart, *The Sexual Man*, 204.

CHAPTER 9: A THEOLOGY OF MODESTY

1. *Merriam Webster's Collegiate Dictionary*, 11th ed., s.v. "modesty."

2. Wendy Shalit, *A Return to Modesty: Discovering the Lost Virtue* (New York: Touchstone, 2000), 97.

3. Ibid.

4. See Shaunti Christine Feldhahn and Lisa Ann Rice, *For Young Women Only: What You Need to Know About How Guys Think* (Sisters, OR: Multnomah Publishers, 2006) and a large portion of Nancy Leigh DeMoss, *The Look: Does God Really Care What I Wear?* (Buchanan, MI: Revive Our Hearts, 2003).

5. This argument seems verified by psychology but not by the Bible and breeds an allowance for "visual sin" that has crept into Christian culture. Men are continually told they are "visual" and one begins to think this means they would shield their eyes; however, it seems to make allowance for looking, a "boys will be boys" attitude.

6. 1 Tim. 2:9

7. Some may argue that Adam and Eve were not "technically" married. For treatment on this subject please see Eph. 5:29–32.

8. Gen. 2:25

9. Gen. 3:7

10. Nancy Leigh De Moss, *The Look*, 11.

11. Gen. 3:11

12. In our post-fall world there is an appropriate place for nakedness. God has given us redemption through union with Christ and union with our spouses. In marriage we can be naked—this is a great and good gift. Our desire to be desired, to be seen, to be known, can be fulfilled in marriage. God does not leave us craving the garden; instead, He provides a way to have what Adam and Eve had together, post-fall.

13. Rom. 13:14

14. Gal. 3:27

15. As a rudimentary definition, we'll define "dualism" as dividing something in two, in this case, dividing physical and spiritual selves.

16. Some of us play the beauty card to compensate for our insecurities. I'd be lying if I wasn't in that camp more often than I care to admit: makeup, shirts and pants that show off "all the right angles." However, insecurity does not give license to relevancy or modification for the sake of fitting in. Feeling poorly about ourselves does not give us free reign to be immodest—even if it "makes us feel better."

17. Rebecca Konyndyk DeYoung, *Glittering Vices* (Grand Rapids: Brazos Press, 2009), 163.

CHAPTER 10: IS IT WORTH IT? IS HE WORTHY?

1. *The American Heritage Dictionary*, 2nd College ed., s.v. "worthy."

2. Ann Spangler, "Preface," *Bright Legacy: Portraits of Ten Outstanding Christian Women*, edited by Ann Spangler (Ann Arbor, Mi: Servant Books, 1983), 1–2.

3. Kathryn Stockett, *The Help* (New York: Berkeley Books, 2009), 73–74.

4. Carolyn G. Heilbrun, *Writing a Woman's Life* (New York: W. W. Norton and Co., 1988), 128.

5. C. S. Lewis, *The Four Loves* (New York: Harcourt, Brace, Jovanovich, 1960), 87–89, 93, 104, 111.

6. Eugene Peterson, *Leap over a Wall* (Harper/San Francisco, 1997), 53.

7. Dietrich Bonhoeffer, *Life Together* (New York: HarperOne, 1978), 54–55, 37.

8. Flannery O'Connor, "A Temple of the Holy Ghost," *Three* (New York: A Signet Book, 1962), 185.

APPENDIX 2: "SO MUCH FROM SO LITTLE"

1. Wendy Shalit, *A Return to Modesty: Discovering the Lost Virtue* (New York: Touchstone, 2000), 94–95.

2. Ibid., 172.

3. Ibid., 182.

4. Ibid., 186–87.

RESOURCES

**Many of the works of fiction titles provided, most of them
but not all written by women, address issues pertinent to
women, raise thought-provoking questions, and/or present
female protagonists whose decisions, for good or bad, have
crucial consequences.**

Angelou, Maya. *I Know Why the Caged Bird Sings*

Austen, Jane. *Emma, Persuasion, Pride and Prejudice, Sense and
Sensibility*

Brontë, Anne. *The Tenant of Wildfell Hall*

Brontë, Charlotte. *Jane Eyre, Shirley, Villette*

Buck, Pearl. *The Good Earth*

Cather, Willa. *My Antonia*

Chopin, Kate. *The Awakening*

Eliot, George. *The Mill on the Floss, Middlemarch*

Flaubert, Gustave. *Madame Bovary*

Gaskell, Elizabeth. *Ruth*

Golds, Cassandra. *The Museum of Mary Child*

Hartman, Olov. *Holy Masquerade*

James, Henry. *Washington Square, The Portrait of a Lady*

Lee, Harper. *To Kill a Mockingbird*

Lewis, C. S. *Till We Have Faces, The Great Divorce, The Screwtape
Letters*

Lowry, Lois. *Number the Stars* (about friendship)

MacDonald, George. *The Wise Woman* (children's story that shows the
discipline of God through a wise woman in two young girls' lives)

Marshall, Catherine. *Christy*

Morrison, Toni. *The Bluest Eye*
Samson, Lisa. *Quaker Summer*
Schaefer, Jack. *Shane* (wonderful model of a Christlike man)
See, Lisa. *Snow Flower and the Secret Fan*
Smith, Betty. *A Tree Grows in Brooklyn*
Thackeray, William. *Vanity Fair*
Tolstoy, Leo. *Anna Karenina*
Walker, Alice. *The Color Purple*
Wharton, Edith. *The Age of Innocence, The House of Mirth*

SHORT STORIES
Anderson, Sherwood. "Adventure"
Chopin, Kate. "The Story of an Hour", "Désirée's Baby"
Dinesen, Isak. "Babette's Feast"
Fitzgerald, F, Scott. "A New Leaf"
Freeman, Mary Wilkins. "The Revolt of 'Mother'"
Gilman, Charlotte Perkins. "The Yellow Wallpaper"
Glaspell, Susan. "A Jury of Her Peers"
Hemingway, Ernest. "Hills Like White Elephants"
Kingston, Maxine Hong. "No-Name Woman"
O'Connor, Flannery. "The Temple of the Holy Ghost"

MOVIES
Age of Innocence
An Education
Babette's Feast
Emma
Everafter
Jane Eyre (2011)
Persuasion

Pride and Prejudice
Rabbit-Proof Fence
Sense and Sensibility
Shadowlands
Sophie Scholl
The Color Purple
The Inn of the Sixth Happiness (story of missionary Gladys Aylward)
The Joy That Kills (based on "The Story of an Hour")
The Nativity Story
Washington Square
Yentl

NONFICTION

Ashcroft, Mary Ellen. *Temptations Women Face*
Barnes, M. Craig. *Yearning*
Carmichael, Amy. *Rose from Brier, Edges of His Ways*
Curtis, Brent, and John Eldredge. *The Sacred Romance: Drawing Closer to the Heart of God*
Elliot, Elisabeth. *These Strange Ashes*
Fee, Gordon, and Douglas Stuart. *How to Read the Bible for All Its Worth*
Frank, Anne. *The Diary of a Young Girl*
Gire, Ken. *Windows of the Soul*
Guinness, Os. *When No One Sees: The Importance of Character in an Age of Image, Steering Through Chaos: Vice and Virtue in an Age of Moral Confusion*
Hart, Archibald. *The Sexual Man*
http://www.focusministries1.org/books.asp (Headed by Paul Silva website of ministry to abused women, education and practical.)
James, Carolyn Custis. *When Life and Beliefs Collide*

Kilbourne, Jean. *Deadly Persuasion: Why Women and Girls Must Fight
the Addictive Power of Advertising.* Now called *Can't Buy My* Love

Lewis, C. S. *The Weight of Glory and Other Addresses*

Mathews, Alice. *A Woman God Can Use: Lessons from Old Testament
Women to Help You Make Today's Choices, Preaching That Speaks
to Women*

Plantinga, Cornelius, Jr. *Not the Way It's Supposed to Be: A Breviary
of Sin*

Radway, Janice. *Reading the Romance: Women, Patriarchy, and
Popular Culture*

Roseveare, Helen. *He Gave Us a Valley, Living Sacrifice*

Ryken, Leland. *Triumphs of the Imagination: Literature in Christian
Perspective*

Sayers, Dorothy. *Are Women Human?*

Scott, Sandra. *Charmers and Con Artists: And Their Flip Side*

Shalit, Wendy. *A Return to Modesty: Discovering the Lost Virtue*

Sumner, Sarah. *Men and Women in Ministry*

Winter, Richard. *Still Bored in a Culture of Entertainment*

SEXUAL ISSUES

Ferree, Marnie C. *No Stones: Women Redeemed from Sexual Addiction*

Hallman, Janelle. *The Heart of Female Same-Sex Attraction*

Hollinger, Dennis P. *The Meaning of Sex: Christian Ethics and the
Moral Life*

Paulk, Anne. *Restoring Sexual Identity: Hope for Women Who Struggle
with Same-Sex Attraction*

Trobisch, Walter and Ingrid. *My Beautiful Feeling: Correspondence
with Ilona*

Winner, Lauren. *Real Sex*

ACKNOWLEDGMENTS

This book would never have been written if it had not been for the firm initial encouragement of a number of people in the face of my significant reluctance. I owe Paul Santhouse, former student and now a colleague, a great deal. For years he urged me to write a manuscript and even gave me suggestions as to what to write about. A group of students (Katelyn McNeil, Corum Hughes, Ashley High, Lee Anna Smith, and Parker Hathaway) from his publishing class were commissioned to get contracts as part of their experience. Katelyn McNeill was the first to approach me with great energy, and in a weak moment I said yes. This group, as I understand it, presented my ideas with enthusiasm to the Moody Publishers' team. Later on, a number of other students worked on the trailer for the book with great attention to detail: they were Alexis Berry, Crystal Anderson, Morgan Sutter, Matt Snyder, John McPherson, Emily Pine, and C. W. Allen. Rachel Rounds helped with promotion.

I am also indebted to the three other writers who agreed to write chapters for the book, filling in the gaps in my treatment of the theme. These include Stacy Parlee-Johnson, Pam MacRae, and Linda Haines. Pam consistently expressed her belief in the theme and content, and gave perspective on details. Linda talked me through the process from start to finish including structural design, content, and expression. She often led me to sources, helped me to refine my thinking, and admonished me to infuse my strong point of view with grace.

As I was writing, a number of students conducted informal surveys and were available to interact with my questions. I am grateful to Lana Norris, Haley Holik, Megan Toth, and Heather Zimmerman for their input. A warm and personal thank-you also goes to Amy Koehler, my colleague in the library, for so many kindnesses including her willingness to read and critique the manuscript late in the game and for putting together the endnotes (a substantial endeavor) not to mention her numerous thoughtful and wise notes throughout the last hard weeks of writing.

Of course, Randall Payleitner was there at every turn of the road with ready replies, guidance, encouragement, and strong leadership. Thanks to Duane Sherman for help with the cover and to Betsey Newenhuyse, my editor, for her intelligent interaction in the process of bringing the manuscript to publication.

Finally, I must express gratitude to my parents. My mother taught me the love of books and education from the time I could lisp, and she read to me tirelessly much of my childhood. She was also a defender, helper, and teacher of women, encouraging them to have a sense of voice. My father was an honorable and wise man of enduring faith who always treated women as equals and who taught me to respect myself.